AFRICAN POLITICAL, ECONOMIC, AND SECURITY ISSUES

MOROCCO

CONDITIONS, ISSUES, AND FOREIGN RELATION

AFRICAN POLITICAL, ECONOMIC, AND SECURITY ISSUES

Additional books in this series can be found on Nova's website under the Series tab.

Additional e-books in this series can be found on Nova's website under the eBooks tab.

AFRICAN POLITICAL, ECONOMIC, AND SECURITY ISSUES

MOROCCO

CONDITIONS, ISSUES, AND FOREIGN RELATION

WILSON GRAVES
EDITOR

nova publishers
New York

NOTICE TO THE READER

Additional color graphics may be available in the e-book version of this book.

Library of Congress Cataloging-in-Publication Data

ISBN: 978-1-63485-107-7

Published by Nova Science Publishers, Inc. † New York

CONTENTS

PREFACE

Successive U.S. Administrations have viewed Morocco as an important regional ally, a partner in counterterrorism, and a free trade counterpart. Morocco receives substantial U.S. development aid, and bilateral trade and investment have increased following a 2006 Free Trade Agreement. Morocco also benefits from U.S. security assistance and military cooperation, and is a purchaser of U.S. defense articles, including F-16 jets. Some observers have placed greater emphasis on the U.S.-Morocco relationship amid regional turmoil and terrorist threats emanating from neighboring states in North Africa and the nearby Sahel region of West Africa. This book discusses current issues in Morocco. It also focuses on the geopolitical and economic drivers for the renewed Moroccan interest in West Africa and examines how Morocco is conducting its foreign and security policy in a variety of Western African countries. Furthermore, the book includes Morocco's 2014 Human Rights Report, International Religious Freedom Report, and the Investment Climate Statement for 2015.

In: Morocco
Editor: Wilson Graves

ISBN: 978-1-63485-107-7

Chapter 1

MOROCCO: CURRENT ISSUES*

Alexis Arieff

SUMMARY

Successive U.S. Administrations have viewed Morocco as an important regional ally, a partner in counterterrorism, and a free trade counterpart. Morocco receives substantial U.S. development aid, and bilateral trade and investment have increased following a 2006 Free Trade Agreement. Morocco also benefits from U.S. security assistance and military cooperation, and is a purchaser of U.S. defense articles, including F-16 jets. Some observers have placed greater emphasis on the U.S.-Morocco relationship amid regional turmoil and terrorist threats emanating from neighboring states in North Africa and the nearby Sahel region of West Africa. The United States and Morocco initiated a Bilateral Strategic Dialogue in 2012, and King Mohammed VI undertook an official state visit to Washington, DC, in November 2013, his first since 2004.

King Mohammed VI, who inherited the throne in 1999, retains supreme political power in Morocco but has taken some liberalizing steps. In 2011, amid popular demonstrations that echoed unrest elsewhere in the region, the king backed a new constitution that was then adopted by referendum. Provisions in the new constitution could strengthen the legislature, judiciary, and local-level government, if fully implemented. It

* This is an edited, reformatted and augmented version of a Congressional Research Service publication RS21579, prepared for Members and Committees of Congress, dated January 15, 2015.

nonetheless preserves the king's role as the arbiter of political decision-making, head of the military, and the country's highest religious authority. Legislative elections held in 2011, the first under the new constitution, brought an Islamist political party, the Justice and Development Party (PJD), to power for the first time. The PJD has sought to bolster the power of elected officials and to institute economic and governance reforms. However, the party has faced challenges in transitioning from an outsider opposition role to the day-to-day responsibility of policymaking. It has also struggled to overcome tensions with pro-palace elites, as well as with nominal allies. Public protests have dwindled since their peak in 2011, but sporadic demonstrations continue over economic and social grievances, while some Moroccans continue to call for deeper political changes.

With regard to the disputed territory of Western Sahara, which Morocco considers an integral part of its sovereign territory, the United States has recognized neither Morocco's claim to the region, nor the self-declared independent Sahrawi Arab Democratic Republic (SADR), which is backed and hosted by Algeria. U.S. policy over the past decade has been to support U.N.-facilitated negotiations over the territory's final status. Congressional views of the Western Sahara issue have been stated in foreign aid appropriations legislation. Most recently, the Consolidated and Further Continuing Appropriations Act, 2015 (P.L. 113-235, Division J, section 7041[g][1]) states that funds appropriated for foreign bilateral economic assistance "shall be made available for assistance for the Western Sahara." It has been the policy of successive Administrations that funds appropriated for bilateral aid for Morocco may not be programmed in Western Sahara, as doing so could represent a tacit acknowledgment of Moroccan sovereignty. The executive branch interpretation of the FY2015 provision, and its implications, remain to be seen.

Morocco's foreign policy focuses on its Western partners (especially France, Spain, the European Union, and the United States); the Middle East; and francophone Africa. The Moroccan military has reportedly participated in U.S.-led operations to counter the Islamic State organization in Syria. Neighboring Algeria is a regional rival and supports independence for Western Sahara. Friction over the Western Sahara issue has stymied Moroccan-Algerian relations, Moroccan relations with the African Union (Morocco withdrew in 1984 over recognition of the SADR), and regional economic and security cooperation.

Overview

Obama Administration officials have expressed strong support for the Moroccan monarchy, while also encouraging political reforms and occasionally voicing human rights concerns. U.S. bilateral aid assists Morocco with economic growth, basic education, democratization, military and police professionalization, and counterterrorism. In addition, a five-year, $697.5 million U.S. Millennium Challenge Corporation (MCC) compact was completed in September 2013, and Morocco is eligible for a second compact. U.S.-Moroccan military cooperation includes sizable Moroccan purchases of U.S. defense materiel and a large annual bilateral exercise, African Lion.

Amid widespread political upheaval in the region since 2011, Moroccan officials have urged the United States to expand bilateral ties. A U.S.-Morocco Bilateral Strategic Dialogue was initiated in 2012, with working groups devoted to political, economic, security, and educational/cultural cooperation. (Strategic Dialogues were also initiated with Algeria and Tunisia.) High-level sessions of the Dialogue have been held in both countries, most recently in April 2014 in Morocco, with Secretary of State John Kerry leading the U.S. delegation. King Mohammed VI conducted an official state visit to Washington, DC, in November 2013, his first since 2004. The king met with President Obama at the White House, and a joint statement emphasized shared support for Morocco's "democratic and economic reforms" and for bilateral cooperation in a number of domains.[1] In November 2014, Vice President Joe Biden visited Morocco for the Global Entrepreneurship Summit and also met with the king.

With regard to the disputed territory of Western Sahara, the United States has recognized neither Morocco's claim of sovereignty nor the self-proclaimed independent government-in-exile, the Sahrawi Arab Democratic Republic (SADR), which is hosted and supported by Algeria. At the same time—in the context of valued bilateral ties with Morocco—the Obama Administration, using phrasing similar to that employed by the George W. Bush Administration, refers to Morocco's proposal for regional autonomy under Moroccan sovereignty as a "serious, realistic, and credible" potential approach to the territory's final status. U.S. policy over the past decade has been to support United Nations (U.N.)-facilitated negotiations between Morocco and the independence-seeking Popular Front for the Liberation of Saqiat al Hamra and Rio de Oro (Polisario, which formed the SADR) toward a mutually accepted settlement.[2]

In April 2014, the House Foreign Affairs Committee, Subcommittee on the Middle East and North Africa, held a hearing on U.S. policy toward Morocco. Several other hearings during the 113th Congress also examined U.S. policy interests in Morocco and the wider North Africa region.[3] Congressional views on Morocco and the Western Sahara issue have been expressed in foreign aid appropriations legislation (see "Recent Congressional Actions").

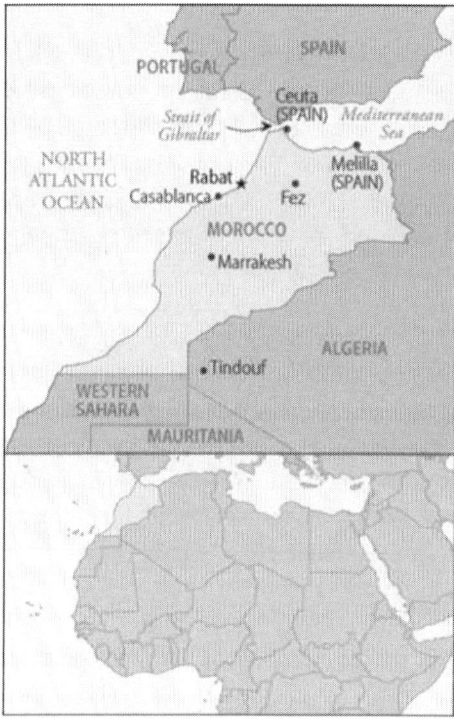

MOROCCO AT A GLANCE

Population: 33 million
Ethnic Groups: Arab-Berber 99%, other 1%
Languages: Arabic (official), Tamazight (official) and other Berber languages, French
Religions: Muslim 99% (official, virtually all Sunni), other 1%
GDP Growth/GDP Per Capita: 3.5% / $3,392
Life Expectancy: 76.5 years
Median Age: 28.1 years
Literacy: 67% (male 76%, female 58%) (2011 est.)
Unemployment: 9.5% (2013 est.); youth ages 15-24, 18.6% (2012)
Female Labor Participation Rate (% of female population): 27% (2013)
Urban Population (% of total): 59%
Key Exports/Top Export Partners: clothing and textiles, electric components, inorganic chemicals, transistors, crude minerals, fertilizers, petroleum products, citrus fruits, vegetables, fish / France, Spain, Brazil, India, United States (2012)
Key Imports/Import Partners: crude petroleum, textile fabric, telecommunications equipment, wheat, gas and electricity, transistors, plastics / Spain, France, China, United States, Saudi Arabia (2012)

Created by CRS. Map boundaries from Map Resources. At-a-glance info from CIA World Factbook; World Bank; International Monetary Fund. Figures are 2014 estimates unless otherwise noted. Map boundaries are not necessarily authoritative.

Note: Morocco considers Western Sahara to be part of its national territory, but U.S. government maps do not include it as such. See, e.g., U.S. Department of State, "Morocco," at http://www.state.gov/p/nea/ci/mo/index.htm.

Figure 1. Morocco at a Glance.

GOVERNMENT AND POLITICS

The Moroccan royal dynasty has ruled the country since the mid-17th century, remaining relatively intact under French and Spanish colonial protectorates.[4] King Mohammed VI, who inherited the Moroccan throne in 1999, is the preeminent state authority within a complex political system that also includes an elected parliament and local-level representatives. The king has said that he is committed to building a democracy, and in 2011 he introduced a new constitution (later adopted in a popular referendum) that, if fully implemented, could strengthen the legislature, the judiciary, and local-level government. The constitution, however, preserves the king's role as the ultimate arbiter of state decision-making, head of the military, and Morocco's highest religious authority. Although the constitution grants some executive powers to a head of government (prime minister), the king approves and may dismiss cabinet ministers. He may also dissolve parliament, call elections, and exercise certain powers via decree. The king also has a "shadow government" of royal advisors and is tied to significant domestic economic enterprises.

The 2011 constitutional revision and other reforms initiated during the "Arab Spring" did not substantially alter the monarchy's political and economic prerogatives, but they demonstrated responsiveness to public pressures for greater political participation. Many observers argued that in introducing the reforms, the king retained his popular legitimacy and ensured Morocco's continued stability.[5] Ultimately, the degree to which the new constitution leads to significant political changes may depend on how it is interpreted and implemented and the extent to which political parties and other interest groups leverage the political space accorded to them. For example, planned justice sector reforms and decentralization, both nominal priorities of constitutional implementation, have made only halting progress. Constitutional provisions on gender equality and parity, along with civil liberty protections, have yet to be implemented.[6] Protests periodically occur, though they have dwindled in size since their peak in 2011. Some Moroccans continue to call for deeper political changes. Much of the public, however, may have lost any appetite for unrest, in part due to the example of turmoil elsewhere in the region.

The bicameral legislature consists of a 270-seat upper house, the Chamber of Counselors, whose members are indirectly elected to nine-year terms, and a 395-seat lower house, the Chamber of Representatives, whose members are directly elected to five-year terms. Sixty seats (about 15%) in the lower house are reserved for women, and 30 seats are reserved for candidates under 40 years of age (candidates for these seats are elected from a separate national list). A law adopted in 2011 expanded previous quotas for women in local-level elected government positions.[7]

The Party for Justice and Democracy (PJD, also known as *Al Misbah*/The Beacon), an Islamist political party, won a plurality of seats (27%) in the most recent elections for the Chamber of Representatives, in 2011. That election was the country's first under the new constitution, which introduced a requirement for the king to appoint the head of government from the largest party in parliament. The PJD's Abdelilah Benkirane was named Prime

Minister and leads an often fractious multiparty government coalition. In government, the PJD has focused on reforming fiscally burdensome state pension system and subsidy programs; it hopes to replace the latter with targeted aid for poor households. It has also weighed in on cultural, media, justice sector, and educational policies, sometimes with the apparent aim of introducing greater religiosity into the public sphere, although the party's leadership defines its stance as one of moderation.[8]

While the PJD has been legally recognized for two decades, it had not held cabinet positions prior to 2011. Some observers view the PJD as more driven by constituent concerns and more focused on countering corruption than other political parties, and therefore interested in devolving power away from the monarchy and toward elected government. In turn, the PJD has reportedly faced opposition from pro-palace elites.[9] Public perceptions of these dynamics may underlie the personal popularity of Prime Minister Benkirane, despite regular policy setbacks.[10] Still, the PJD has not demanded deep political changes, preferring to reassure the monarchy in tacit exchange for greater acceptance into national politics.[11] The party's influence over policymaking is further constrained by its slim legislative plurality, the role of royal advisors who sit outside of elected government, and economic limitations. Mutual distrust between Moroccan Islamists and liberals has also inhibited political cooperation, despite a potential shared interest in democratization.[12]

In 2013, Prime Minister Benkirane was forced to reshuffle the cabinet after a key coalition member, the Istiqlal (Independence) party, withdrew, leaving the coalition without a majority. After months of stalemate, the National Rally of Independents (RNI), which many observers view as close to the palace, joined the government in its place. In exchange, the PJD relinquished several key portfolios, including the Foreign Ministry. Some observers viewed the PJD as weakened by these events, while others posited that it could capitalize on perceptions that it remains an underdog confronting a system of vested interests.[13]

Several other Islamist movements wield influence while operating outside of formal politics. Religiously conservative Salafist groups, for example, have been alternately targeted and courted by the authorities.[14] The Justice and Charity Organization (JCO or *Al Adl Wal Ihsan*), a domestic Sufi movement, is reportedly Morocco's largest grassroots organization. It opposes the monarchy as un-Islamic and undemocratic, and is therefore banned, but its activities are generally tolerated. The JCO eschews violence and often conveys its views in street demonstrations; it was reportedly a key force, in addition to leftist groups, behind Morocco's 2011 protest movement. Some analysts question whether the JCO might move toward more overt political participation in the wake of the death of its founding leader, Sheikh Abdessalem Yassine, in 2012.[15]

TERRORISM AND COUNTERTERRORISM

Moroccan nationals have been implicated in terrorism abroad, and Morocco has suffered from terrorism at home.[16] Within Morocco, numerous small and reportedly unconnected extremist cells adhering to the Salafiya Jihadiya (Reformist Holy War/"Jihadist") ideology are generally viewed as the top security threat.[17] The deadliest terrorist attack on Moroccan soil occurred in 2003, when 12 suicide bombers reportedly linked to Al Qaeda and the Moroccan Islamic Combatant Group (GICM, after its French acronym) attacked five Western and Jewish targets in Casablanca, killing themselves and 33 others, and injuring more than 100.[18] Several small-scale attacks have occurred more recently, including two suicide attacks near the U.S. consulate and the American Language Center in Casablanca in 2007, and a bombing at a Marrakesh café popular with tourists in 2011. Moroccan authorities regularly report that they have disrupted terrorist cells plotting attacks against Moroccan government, military institutions, foreigners, and tourist sites.

Recruitment of Moroccans by transnational terrorist organizations is a key government concern, as is the return of Moroccan nationals who have joined terrorist groups abroad. Some 1,500 Moroccan nationals have reportedly traveled to Syria and Iraq as "foreign fighters," making Morocco one of the largest sources of such combatants, according to statistics published in news reports.[19] Foreign fighters also reportedly include Europeans of Moroccan origin.[20] A Moroccan-led Islamist extremist group operating in Syria, *Harakat Sham al Islam* (Islamic Movement of the Levant), was reportedly founded by three Moroccans who had been detained at Guantánamo and were released to Moroccan custody between 2004 and 2006.[21] Moroccan authorities claim to have disrupted domestic plots by cells affiliated with the Islamic State and other terrorist groups; in November 2014, a previously unknown Morocco-based group calling itself *Jund al Khilafah* (Soldiers of the Caliphate) posted an Internet video pledging allegiance to the Islamic State.

Al Qaeda in the Islamic Maghreb (AQIM), a regional network of Algerian origin and a U.S.- designated Foreign Terrorist Organization (FTO), has carried out attacks in neighboring countries—as have several of its splinter factions and affiliated groups—but not in Morocco to date. In 2014, a State Department official stated in congressional testimony that Morocco's "holistic counterterrorism strategy" had made it "difficult for AQIM to effectively establish a foothold in Morocco."[22] AQIM has nonetheless attempted to recruit Moroccans and has called for attacks in the country.[23] In 2013, the group released a 41-minute video assailing the Moroccan monarchy.

The State Department characterizes Morocco as "a long-standing and effective partner" in counterterrorism.[24] In addition to international cooperation, Morocco's counterterrorism efforts include vigilant security measures, law enforcement efforts, and counter-radicalization programs. Morocco exercises control over religious leaders and institutions and has created theological councils, supervised and trained imams, closed unregulated mosques, retrained some individuals convicted of terror-related crimes to correct their understanding of Islam, and used media efforts to transmit, as one analyst frames it, "a Moroccan Islam that can compete with political Islamists, salafists, and extremists."[25] Morocco has also sought to transmit these values to partner states in West Africa through religious education outreach and exchanges.

Morocco adopted a broad antiterrorism law after the 2003 terrorist attacks in Casablanca, and a new law in 2014 broadened the scope of terrorism offenses amid rising concerns over possible activities by Islamic State sympathizers. Human rights advocates argue that these laws define terrorism too broadly and contain insufficient civil liberties protections.[26] The State Department reports that Morocco's counterterrorism approach "has emphasized adherence to human rights standards and the increased transparency of law enforcement procedures."[27]

In 2011, three European aid workers were kidnapped from the Polisario-administered Western Sahara refugee camps in Tindouf, Algeria, by the Movement for Unity and Jihad in West Africa, an AQIM splinter faction.[28] In reports on the Western Sahara issue, the U.N. Secretary-General has cited concerns about rising insecurity on the eastern side of the berm that demarcates Moroccan-administered areas (to the west) from those controlled by the Polisario.[29] Moroccan officials and some analysts regularly cite fears that an independent Western Sahara would be vulnerable to terrorist and criminal infiltration; some contend that the Polisario itself has links to terrorism. In April 2014, then-Deputy Assistant Secretary of State for Near Eastern Affairs William V. Roebuck testified before Congress that, "We are not aware of links between, for example, the Polisario, and terrorist organizations."[30]

Human Rights

The U.S.-based organization Freedom House rates Morocco's degree of political and civil liberties as "partly free." The State Department reports that "most significant" human rights problems in Morocco are "the lack of citizens' right to change the constitutional provisions establishing the country's monarchical form of government, corruption in all branches of government, and widespread disregard for the rule of law by security forces."[31] Laws barring acts deemed harmful to the monarchy or to Morocco's claim of sovereignty over Western Sahara limit freedom of expression, assembly, and association.[32] U.N. experts have also expressed concern over the reported use of torture to obtain confessions in criminal cases, a lack of due process for those held in pretrial detention, and Morocco's sweeping anti-terrorism legislation.[33] Religious freedom is subject to a prohibition of proselytization to Muslims, and some Moroccan Christians report police harassment.[34] Moroccan officials often dispute critical reports by human rights activists, while noting a commitment to improving human rights conditions.[35]

Pro-independence and human rights activists operating in Moroccan-administered Western Sahara reportedly face particular state restrictions on their freedom of speech, press, assembly, and association; the use of arbitrary and prolonged detention to quell dissent; and detainee abuse.[36] After human rights groups, including the state-backed National Human Rights Council (CNDH), criticized the use of military tribunals to try civilian detainees accused of committing violence during protests in Western Sahara in 2010, the king promised to end the practice. However, the status of legal reforms introduced in 2014 remains uncertain, and the courts reportedly have not investigated detainee allegations of police torture and coerced confessions.[37]

Morocco is a transit point and destination for migrants seeking asylum, economic opportunities, or access to Europe via Spanish enclaves on Morocco's northern coast. Morocco's treatment of African migrants, which has reportedly included large-scale expulsions into desert areas, has been widely criticized. In September 2013, the government announced a new migration and asylum policy that promised an end of expulsions and potential legal status. In early 2014, Human Rights Watch reported that summary expulsions appeared to have ceased under the new policy, but that migrants were still subject to abuse by state security forces.[38]

King Mohammed VI has backed several major initiatives in select areas of human rights. In 2004, the king supported and parliament adopted significant changes to the Family Code, or *Moudawana*, that aimed to improve women's legal rights and socio-economic status. The king also created an Equity and Reconciliation Commission to provide an historical record of state abuses before King Mohammed VI ascended the throne in 1999, to account for the "disappeared," and to compensate victims. He has furthermore attempted to recognize and expand the cultural and linguistic rights of ethnic Berber communities, considered the indigenous inhabitants of North Africa. While recognizing these initiatives as important precedents, however, some human rights advocates have criticized them as insufficient or insufficiently implemented.[39]

THE ECONOMY

Morocco's economy is relatively diverse: key sectors include agriculture, tourism, mining, and textiles and apparel. Remittances from emigrant workers, mainly in Europe, provide another source of foreign exchange and a social safety net. Through internal and Western Saharan mines, Morocco controls some 75% of world reserves of phosphates, which are used in fertilizers—and of which the United States is a top global consumer.[40] Morocco is considered a lower middle income country; poverty and illiteracy remain widespread, especially in rural areas. The unemployment rate is officially 9% but is double that among youth under 24 years old.[41] Socioeconomic hardships drive emigration and occasional unrest. The state has attempted to address discontent through social programs, public sector hiring initiatives and wage increases, and subsidies. The economy grew by 3.5% in 2014 and is projected to grow 4.7% in 2015.[42]

Morocco actively encourages foreign investment and trade. It has a Free Trade Agreement (FTA) and bilateral investment treaty with the United States; an Association Agreement with the European Union; FTAs with several other countries in the Middle East and North Africa; and several free-trade zones. It has also recently positioned itself as a platform for global trade and investment in Sub-Saharan Africa. However, bureaucratic red tape, corruption, high labor costs, opaque regulation, and taxation policies are reportedly constraints on competitiveness.[43]

In 2012, Morocco and the International Monetary Fund (IMF) agreed to a $6.2 billion, two-year line of credit aimed at proactively reassuring investors. Morocco did not end up drawing on the "Precautionary and Liquidity Line," but the IMF concluded that it had "provided useful insurance against external risks while anchoring the authorities' reform agenda and sending positive signals to markets."[44] A two-year successor arrangement with a $5 billion line of credit was agreed to in July 2014. The IMF has praised efforts under the current PJD-led government to reduce Morocco's fiscal deficit, while continuing to call for further reforms "to stabilize the economy, strengthen competitiveness, and build the foundation for stronger and more inclusive growth."[45]

The royal family's role in the economy is reportedly extensive. The phosphate industry and much of the economy are dominated by the royal family and associated elites who control large, multisectoral holding companies. In 2009, King Mohammed VI was reported to be one of the world's 15 richest royal figures, even as Morocco is a relatively poor country; in 2014, *Forbes* estimated his net worth at $2 billion.[46] The royal family reportedly controls a majority stake in the National Investment Company (SNI), which has significant financial, insurance, construction, and commodity interests.[47] The king is also a major landowner.

Morocco meets most of its energy needs by importing oil and gas. It hopes to find offshore oil, which is currently under exploration, including off the coast of Western Sahara (see below). Morocco has also sought to develop domestic renewable energy sources, with a particular focus on solar energy, which it hopes to use domestically and export to Europe.

WESTERN SAHARA[48]

The dispute between Morocco and the independence-seeking Polisario over the former Spanish colony south of Morocco remains unresolved. Morocco occupies some 85% of the territory,[49] which it considers its southern provinces. Morocco says it will only accept a solution that guarantees it sovereignty over "the whole of its territories" and will only negotiate on that basis. A U.N. peacekeeping operation, MINURSO, originally conceived to oversee a referendum on the final status of the region, monitors a 1991 ceasefire between Morocco and the Polisario. Morocco has authorized foreign oil companies to explore off the Saharan coast, and the prospect of discoveries, as yet unrealized, may have hardened its resolve to retain the region.[50]

Talks between Morocco and the Polisario on the final status of the territory are ongoing under the auspices of the Personal Envoy of the U.N. Secretary General for the Western Sahara, Christopher Ross, a U.S. diplomat. In 2007, King Mohammed VI submitted an autonomy plan for Western Sahara, asserting Moroccan sovereignty, to the United Nations. In line with this initiative, the king has pursued policies of decentralization that he says are intended to empower residents of his Saharan provinces. Neither Morocco nor the Polisario has shown interest in a compromise; Morocco contends that autonomy is itself a compromise. The stalemate appears likely to endure.

FOREIGN POLICY

Morocco's foreign policy focuses on its Western partners, the Middle East, and Sub-Saharan Africa.[51] In addition to Morocco's Foreign Minister, Salaheddine Mezouar, who is from the RNI party, the king and his royal advisors play a key role in foreign policy; they have prioritized close ties with the West while Prime Minister Benkirane has occasionally publicly criticized Western policies.[52] The European Union (EU) is Morocco's top trading partner and provides considerable aid. European leaders appear to hope that Morocco's stability will be preserved amid regional upheaval. They also seek Moroccan cooperation to stem illegal immigration and drug trafficking via Morocco to Europe. Morocco's EU Association Agreement entered into force in 2000, and a 2012 trade agreement expanded the duty-free treatment of agricultural, food, and fisheries products on both sides. A new fishing agreement that includes European access to the coastline of disputed Western Sahara was ratified in 2014, after a hiatus; the previous agreement was discontinued in 2011 due to some EU parliamentarians' objections to conditions in Moroccan-administered Western Sahara, as well as environmental and economic concerns.

Diplomatic, commercial, and military ties with former colonial powers France and Spain are extensive, and both countries have large immigrant populations of Moroccan origin. Frictions with France nonetheless arose in 2014 over allegations by France-based Moroccan activists of torture in Morocco; statements critical of Morocco that were attributed in the press to a senior French diplomat; and, possibly, France's recent cultivation of closer ties with Algeria.[53] After the January 2015 terrorist attacks in France, Foreign Minister Mezouar declined to attend France's multinational rally against extremism due to the presence of "blasphemous caricatures of the Prophet."[54] Spain, for its part, possesses two territorial enclaves on Morocco's Mediterranean coast, Ceuta and Melilla, which Morocco claims, sometimes causing bilateral tensions. The neighbors also have an unresolved dispute concerning territorial waters between Morocco and the Spanish Canary Islands in the Atlantic Ocean. Still, territorial disputes and occasional criticism by

Spanish politicians of Morocco's stance on Western Sahara appear secondary to economic, security, and law enforcement cooperation.

Morocco positions itself as a moderate Arab state and has sought to play a role in addressing conflicts in the Middle East. In recent years, it has drawn closer to fellow Arab monarchies in the Gulf, which have offered aid, investment, and security cooperation. Morocco broke diplomatic relations with the Syrian government in 2012, and the Moroccan military has reportedly participated in U.S.-led military operations against the Islamic State.[55] The king supports a two-state solution to the Israeli-Palestinian conflict and chairs the Al Quds (Jerusalem) Committee of the Organization of the Islamic Conference, which seeks to bolster Muslim claims to the city. The king recognized President Mahmoud Abbas as the legitimate leader of the Palestinian people in Abbas's dispute with Hamas and has urged Palestinian national unity. Morocco closed Israel's liaison bureau in Morocco and Morocco's office in Tel Aviv during the Palestinian *intifada* (uprising) in 2001. Still, links between the two countries remain, as some 600,000 Israelis are of Moroccan origin, and thousands travel to Morocco yearly.

Morocco and Algeria are regional rivals. The two countries fought a war over disputed border territories in 1963-1964, and the border was not demarcated until 1972. It has been closed by Algeria since 1994, after Morocco imposed visa restrictions on Algerian nationals and blamed Algeria for a terrorist attack. The Western Sahara is a key element of bilateral tensions. Moroccan officials frequently indicate their belief that Algeria could solve the Western Sahara issue if it wanted, presumably by pressuring the Polisario, while Algeria argues it is not a party to a dispute that it characterizes as between two sovereign nations (Western Sahara and Morocco). The dispute over the territory of Western Sahara has stymied Moroccan-Algerian relations, Moroccan relations with the African Union (AU), and regional economic and security cooperation.[56]

U.S. Relations

The United States and Morocco have long-term, warm relations; Morocco's monarchy was one of the first governments to recognize the independence of the United States.[57] In 2004, then-President George W. Bush designated Morocco a Major Non-NATO ally. The U.S.-Morocco relationship focuses on promoting regional stability, supporting democratic reform efforts, countering violent extremism, and strengthening trade and cultural ties.[58] The

Bilateral Strategic Dialogue initiated in 2012 has resulted in the enumeration of shared commitments in a number of areas, such as implementation of Morocco's new constitution, the promotion of economic growth in Morocco, and coordination on criminal justice, nonproliferation, and counterterrorism.

Bilateral ties have been enhanced by security cooperation and assistance. Over 1,000 U.S. personnel participate annually in a flagship bilateral military exercise, African Lion, and smaller bilateral exercises are held regularly. Recent Moroccan purchases of U.S. defense materiel include 24 F-16 aircraft; 24 T-6 trainer aircraft; 90 AGM-D Maverick air-to-ground missiles; refurbishment worth over $1 billion for 200 Abrams M1A1 tanks acquired as a grant U.S. transfer; advanced AM 120-C7 air-to-air medium-range missiles systems; and Joint Direct Attack Munition (JDAM) missile guidance kits.[59] Sales agreements for U.S.-made military radar systems and Sidewinder missiles were announced in 2011. Morocco is also a top recipient of U.S. Excess Defense Articles (EDA) grants, and a U.S. National Guard State Partnership Program with Utah was established in 2003. Morocco is part of NATO's Mediterranean Dialogue, has hosted and participated in NATO military exercises, and cooperates with NATO's Operation Active Endeavor, monitoring the Mediterranean Sea for terrorists.

A U.S.-Morocco free trade agreement (FTA) came into effect on January 1, 2006 (P.L. 108-302), eliminating duties on over 95% of all goods and services.[60] Since then, U.S. exports to Morocco have nearly tripled in value, and U.S. imports from Morocco have nearly doubled.[61] However, the agreement has been controversial in Morocco, particularly among labor leaders, and Prime Minister Benkirane suggested in a 2012 address to parliament that Morocco was not sufficiently benefitting from it. Morocco was the United States' 69th-largest goods trading partner in 2013 (latest available): U.S. exports to Morocco in 2013 were valued at $2.48 billion, and U.S. imports from Morocco at $977 million.[62] The United States and Morocco signed new trade agreements under the FTA in December 2012 and November 2013, and a Customs Mutual Assistance Agreement in November 2013.

As noted above ("Overview"), the United States has not recognized Morocco's claim of sovereignty over Western Sahara, nor has it recognized the Polisario's self-proclaimed independent government-in-exile, the SADR. The Obama Administration refers to Morocco's proposal to grant Western Sahara autonomy under Moroccan sovereignty as "a serious, realistic, and credible proposal" and "a potential approach that could satisfy the aspirations of the people in the Western Sahara to run their own affairs in peace and dignity."[63] At the same time, it maintains that the parties "have to reach a mutually agreed upon solution" through negotiations and that the United States cannot "impose" a solution.[64] U.S.-Morocco relations were briefly troubled in April 2013 by U.S. support in the U.N. Security Council for adding human rights monitoring to MINURSO's mandate. Morocco vehemently objects to a human rights monitoring role for the mission as an affront to its sovereignty. Ultimately, the proposal did not advance.

U.S. Assistance

The United States provides aid to Morocco to help advance democratization, alleviate poverty, increase military effectiveness, counter terrorism, and build trade capacity. The Obama Administration requested $30.9 million in bilateral foreign assistance for Morocco in FY2015 (see *Table 1*), stating that such aid would support Morocco's achievement of "critical" reforms.[65]

The U.S. Agency for International Development (USAID) current five-year strategy for Morocco, which is designed to support Morocco's development and reform objectives, lists three core objectives: increasing youth employability, expanding civic participation in governance, and enhancing the quality of primary school education.[66] USAID activities in Morocco focus on improving agricultural growth and productivity; enhancing teacher training; building the capacity of local-level government to respond to citizen demands; addressing the needs of the most at-risk youth through engagement in productive social, economic, and civic activities; and assisting Moroccan businesses in meeting the requirements of the U.S. Morocco FTA.[67]

In addition to the bilateral aid cited above, Morocco recently benefitted from a five-year, $697.5 million Millennium Challenge Corporation (MCC) compact, which was completed in 2013. It focused on alleviating poverty through targeted investments in fruit tree productivity, fisheries, artisan production, financial services, and private enterprises.[68] Morocco is eligible for a new compact, for which it is developing proposals. In November 2014, the MCC announced that it expected to invest $50 million to improve Morocco's technical and vocational education system as part of a compact agreement "to be signed in 2015," pending MCC Board approval and congressional notification.[69]

Morocco also participates in U.S. regional aid programs, including the Trans-Sahara Counterterrorism Partnership (TSCTP), a State Department-led interagency initiative that includes 11 states in North and West Africa; the

Administration's Middle East and North Africa Transition Fund, which has provided technical aid for good governance; and grants administered by the Middle East Partnership Initiative (MEPI), the State Department's regional democracy-promotion entity, for women's empowerment, civil society, job growth, and legal reforms. Morocco also receives assistance administered by the international financial institutions (such as the IMF and World Bank), which receive U.S. funding.

Morocco has committed resources of its own in support of several U.S.-Morocco cooperation initiatives, including the Peace Corps program in Morocco and a five-year "Virtual Exchange Initiative" named in honor of the late U.S. Ambassador Christopher Stevens, which aims to connect youth in the Middle East/North Africa and the United States.

Table 1. U.S. Bilateral Foreign Assistance to Morocco, Selected Accounts

Appropriations, current $ thousands (State Department and USAID)

	FY2010	FY2011	FY2012	FY2013	FY2014 (estimated)	FY2015 (requested)
ESF	3,000	2,281	0	1,929	20,896	20,000
FMF	9,000	8,982	8,000	7,595	7,000	5,000
IMET	1,789	1,989	1,898	1,677	1,710	1,650
INCLE	750	750	9,000 [of which 7,500 in OCO]	1,500	3,000	3,000
NADR	1,200	1,100	3,300	1,684	1,470	1,250
DA	19,546	19,039	19,039	16,720	0	0
Total	*35,396*	*34,141*	*41,237*	*31,105*	*34,076*	*30,900*

Source: State Department, Congressional Budget Justification for Foreign Operations, FY2012-FY2015.

Notes: (1) FMF=Foreign Military Financing, ESF=Economic Support Funds, IMET=International Military Education and Training, INCLE=International Narcotics Control and Law Enforcement, NADR=Nonproliferation, Antiterrorism, Demining, and Related Activities, DA=Development Assistance, OCO=Overseas Contingency Operations. (2) Table does not include MCC funding or other assistance administered under regional or global programs, or by U.S. departments or agencies other than the State Department and USAID.

Recent Congressional Actions

Many Members of Congress are strongly supportive of the Moroccan government and its stance on Western Sahara, and many have expressed appreciation for King Mohammed VI's reform initiatives. Other Members have expressed concern over Morocco's handling of the Western Sahara issue, and/or over human rights and religious freedom problems. Several hearings in the 113th Congress examined U.S. policy interests in Morocco and North Africa (see "Overview").

The explanatory statement accompanying the FY2015 Department of State, Foreign Operations, and Related Programs Appropriations Act (Division J of P.L. 113-235, the Consolidated and Further Continuing Appropriations Act, 2015) provides $20 million in budget authority for Economic Support Fund (ESF) aid for Morocco (equal to the Administration's bilateral aid request) and $7 million for Foreign Military Financing (FMF) ($2 million more than requested). The explanatory statement "expects that no [FMF] funds will be used for internal security purposes," referring to a provision in the act that FMF funds for Morocco "may only be used for the purposes requested" in the Administration's FY2015 congressional budget justification (Division J, §7041[g][2]). Separately, the explanatory statement appears to endorse a requirement for the State Department to report on why it is not implementing a recommendation by its Office of the Inspector-General to close the U.S. Consulate in Casablanca.[70]

Morocco and the Polisario, and advocates on both sides, regularly appeal to Congress to support their respective positions on Western Sahara. Congressional views on the Western Sahara issue have been stated in official correspondence and in foreign aid appropriations legislation. The FY2014 Consolidated Appropriations Act (Division K of P.L. 113-76, §7041[h]) provided that bilateral economic assistance appropriated for Morocco "should also be available for assistance for the territory of the Western Sahara."[71] It has been the policy of successive Administrations that funds appropriated for bilateral aid for Morocco may not be programmed in Western Sahara, as doing so could represent a tacit acknowledgment of Moroccan sovereignty. The FY2014 provision did not appear to alter this policy in practice.

A modified provision contained in the FY2015 Act (Division J of P.L. 113-235, §7041[g][1]) states that funds appropriated for global bilateral economic assistance "shall be made available for assistance for the Western Sahara." It also requires the State Department to "consult with the Committees on Appropriations on the proposed uses of such funds." The executive branch interpretation of the FY2015 provision, and its implications, remain to be seen.

The explanatory statement accompanying P.L. 113-235 endorses a requirement in S.Rept. 113- 195 for the State Department to update its report to the appropriators on "steps taken during the previous 12 months by the Government of Morocco to release political prisoners and support a human rights monitoring and reporting role for the U.N. Mission in Western Sahara."[72]

OUTLOOK

The United States and Morocco continue to share an interest in promoting stability and pursuing economic and security cooperation amid ongoing regional tumult. Morocco's role in counterterrorism and regional security is likely to remain of interest to Members of Congress, as is the bilateral trade and investment relationship. Congressional efforts to use foreign aid appropriations legislation to prompt the executive branch to change its policy toward the disputed territory of Western Sahara have gained in prominence in recent years. Some Members have also continued to focus on the degree to which U.S. policy toward Morocco includes the encouragement of human rights and democracy. The role of Moroccan Islamist political parties and movements may also be of congressional interest in the context of regional developments.

End Notes

[1] White House, "Joint Statement by the United States of America and the Kingdom of Morocco," November 22, 2013.

[2] See, e.g., testimony of William V. Roebuck, then-Deputy Assistant Secretary of State for Near Eastern Affairs, before the House Foreign Affairs Committee, Subcommittee on the Middle East and North Africa, April 9, 2014.

[3] These included "The Middle East and North Africa FY2014 Budget: Priorities and Challenges," House Foreign Affairs Committee, Subcommittee on the Middle East and North Africa, May 2013; "Political, Economic, and Security Situation in North Africa," Senate Foreign Relations Committee, Subcommittee on Near Eastern and South and Central Asian Affairs, November 2013; and "Political Pluralism in the OSCE [Organization for Security and Cooperation in Europe] Mediterranean Partners?," U.S. Helsinki Commission, July 2014. The U.S. Helsinki Commission, or Commission on Security and Cooperation in Europe, is an independent federal agency that consists of members from the U.S. Senate; the House of Representatives; and the Departments of State, Defense, and Commerce.

[4] Morocco gained independence from France in 1956. Spain retained two coastal enclaves, Ceuta and Melilla.

[5] See, e.g., Aidan Lewis, "Why Has Morocco's King Survived the Arab Spring?" BBC News, November 24, 2011.

[6] State Department, Country Reports on Human Rights Practices for 2013, "Morocco," February 2014; Aida Alamijune, "Morocco's King Slow to Deliver on Pro-Democracy Vows," New York Times, June 11, 2014.

[7] The Quota Project (database), "Morocco," at http://www.quotaproject.org/uid/countryview.cfm?CountryCode=MA.

[8] Institute for Research and Debate on Governance, "Analyse et perspective d'un parti islamique au Maroc" [interview with Lahcen Daoudi], http://www.institut-gouvernance.org/en/entretien/fiche-entretien-55.html.

[9] See, e.g., Africa Confidential, "Headaches for Benkirane," January 24, 2014; Intissar Fakir and Maati Monjib, "Rabat's Undoing," Foreign Affairs, October 23, 2014.

[10] A public opinion poll found in January 2015 that 48% of Moroccans hoped Benkirane would remain the head of government, a significant decrease from 2014 but still 11 points higher than those who preferred he step down. L'Economiste, "Enquête L'Economiste-Sunergia: Benkirane... homme d'Etat," January 6, 2015.

[11] Anouar Boukhars, Morocco's Islamists: Bucking the Trend? FRIDE, June 6, 2014. For example, PJD Prime Minister Abdelilah Benkirane refers to the ruling family as "a referee" in Morocco's political system and defends laws banning criticism of the king. (Benkirane interview with Fareed Zakaria at the World Economic Forum, January 25, 2013.)

[12] Maâti Monjib, The "Democratization" Process in Morocco: Progress, Obstacles, and the Impact of the Islamist-Secularist Divide, Saban Center, Brookings Institution, Working Paper Number 5, August 2011; and Mohammed Masbah, "Islamist-Secularist Divisions in Morocco," Sada, May 29, 2014.

[13] Financial Times, "Morocco: Dance with the Deep State," July 15, 2013; and Ursula Lindsey, "All the King's Men [op-ed]," New York Times, June 5, 2013.

[14] Mohammed Masbah, "Moving Towards Political Participation: The moderation of Moroccan Salafis since the beginning of the Arab Spring," SWP Comments, January 2013. "Salafism" refers to a broad subset of Sunni Islamic reformist movements that seek to purify contemporary Islamic religious practices and societies by encouraging the application of practices and views associated with the earliest days of the Islamic faith. Salafist movements hold a range of positions on political, social, and theological questions. A subset of Salafists advocate violence in pursuit of their aims, but many instead pursue nonviolent preaching, charity, and (for some) political activities. See CRS Report RS21745, Islam: Sunnis and Shiites, by Christopher M. Blanchard.

[15] Vish Sakhthivel, Al-Adl wal-Ihsan: Inside Morocco's Islamist Challenge, Washington Institute for Near East Policy, August 2014.

[16] Noteworthy developments abroad include the trial of two Moroccans in German courts for aiding the 9/11 terrorists and the revelation that a Moroccan imam was "the spiritual father of the Hamburg cell" that helped execute the 9/11 attacks. A French-Moroccan, Zacarias Moussaoui, was tried in the United States as the 20th hijacker for 9/11. A Moroccan network was implicated in the March 2004 Madrid train bombings. In February 2012, a Moroccan national was arrested in Washington, DC, on accusations of plotting to bomb the U.S. Capitol building.

[17] State Department, Country Reports on Terrorism 2013, "Morocco," April 2014.

[18] The attacks occurred after Osama Bin Laden listed Morocco among the "oppressive, unjust, apostate ruling governments," which he characterized as "enslaved by America" and, therefore, "most eligible for liberation." New York Times, "Moroccans Say Al Qaeda Masterminded and Financed Casablanca Suicide Bombings," May 23, 2003. The GICM was also linked to the 2004 Madrid train bombings, and in 2005 the State Department designated the group as a Foreign Terrorist Organization (FTO). However, the GICM has reportedly been inactive since a crackdown on its followers in Europe and elsewhere, and it was de-listed in 2013.

[19] See, e.g., Washington Post, "Foreign Fighters Flow to Syria [Info-Graphic]," October 11, 2014; and The Economist, "It Ain't Half Hot Here, Mum: Why and how Westerners go to fight in Syria and Iraq," August 30, 2014.

[20] Jeffrey D. Palmer, "The Death of Moroccan Exceptionalism: A Brief History of Moroccan Salafi Jihadism and Current Jihadist Trends," Jihadology.net, September 5, 2014.

[21] Two of the three have reportedly been killed in combat. See Maria Abi-Habib, "After Guantanamo, Freed Detainees Returned to Violence in Syria Battlefields," Wall Street Journal, June 3, 2014. See also Mohammed Masbah, "Is AlQaeda a Threat to Moroccan Stability?" Sada, October 2013; and Vish Sakthivel, "Weathering Morocco's Syria Returnees," Washington Institute for Near East Policy, September 2013. In 2014, another Moroccan ex-Guantánamo detainee, who had reportedly been transferred from U.S. to Spanish custody in 2005, was arrested in Spain on accusations of recruiting fighters for the Islamic State.

[22] Statement of William V. Roebuck, then-Deputy Assistant Secretary of State for Near Eastern Affairs, before the House Foreign Affairs Committee, Subcommittee on the Middle East and North Africa, April 9, 2014.

[23] State Department, Country Reports on Terrorism 2013, op. cit.

[24] State Department, Country Reports on Terrorism 2013, op. cit.

[25] Haim Malka, "The Struggle for Religious Identity in Tunisia and the Maghreb," Center for Strategic and International Studies, May 2014.

[26] Agence France Presse (AFP), "UN calls for an end to torture confessions in Morocco," December 18, 2013; Borzou Daragahi, "Spectre of Isis Used to Erode Rights in Morocco," January 4, 2015; Anna Jacobs, "Morocco's Crackdown on Human Rights Groups Divides the Government," Muftah, October 2, 2014. In 2010, Human Rights Watch (HRW) reported a "pattern of abuse" under the 2003 law, including extrajudicial detentions; torture and ill-treatment of detainees; and coerced confessions. Moroccan authorities rejected the report's primary allegations and disputed the details of cases cited in it. HRW, "Morocco: End Abuses in Counterterrorism Arrests," October 25, 2010.

[27] State Department, Country Reports on Terrorism 2013, op. cit.

[28] The hostages were subsequently released, reportedly in exchange for European ransom payments and the release of militants from prison in Mauritania. The Movement for Unity and Jihad in West Africa later merged with another AQIM splinter group to form Al Murabitoun, which is a U.S.-designated FTO.

[29] Report of the Secretary-General on the Situation Concerning Western Sahara, April 10, 2014, U.N. doc. S/2014/258.

[30] Testimony before the House Foreign Affairs Committee, Subcommittee on the Middle East and North Africa, op. cit.

[31] State Department, Country Reports on Human Rights Practices for 2013, "Morocco," February 2014. The report also described "the police use of excessive force to quell peaceful

protests"; pretrial detention and poor prison conditions; the reported existence of "political prisoners"; a lack of judicial independence; and human trafficking.

32 Human Rights Watch (HRW), World Report 2014, "Morocco/Western Sahara." Media advocates contend that, in addition, some prosecutions of critical journalists on charges ostensibly unrelated to their journalism are designed to inhibit independent coverage and commentary, and that financial pressures are employed to quiet some media outlets.

33 AFP, "UN Calls for an End to Torture Confessions in Morocco," December 18, 2013; U.N. doc. A/HRC/22/53/Add.2, Report of the Special Rapporteur on Torture and Other Cruel, Inhuman or Degrading Treatment or Punishment, Mission to Morocco, April 30, 2013.

34 State Department, International Religious Freedom Report for 2013, "Morocco," July 2014. In 2010, the government expelled foreign Christians, including Americans, on allegations of proselytizing.

35 See, for example, U.N. Human Rights Council, U.N. doc. A/HRC/22/53/Add.5, Report of the Special Rapporteur [...], Mission to Morocco: comments by the State on the report of the Special Rapporteur, March 4, 2013.

36 State Department, Country Reports on Human Rights Practices for 2013, "Western Sahara," February 2014.

37 HRW, "Morocco: Sahrawi Activist Facing Military Tribunal: Promised End to Such Trials for Civilians Not Yet a Reality," December 22, 2014; "Morocco/Western Sahara: Fair Trials Elusive: Court Ignores Torture Allegations," September 9, 2014; "Just Sign Here": Unfair Trials Based on Confessions to the Police in Morocco, June 21, 2013.

38 HRW, Abused and Expelled: Ill-Treatment of Sub-Saharan African Migrants in Morocco, February 10, 2014.

39 For example, regarding women's rights, judges have not applied the 2004 law or new constitutional provisions on gender equality consistently, and women reportedly continue to experience discrimination, a lack of equal access to the justice system, and gender-based violence. Some advocates contend that some of the Equity and Reconciliation Commission's recommendations have not been implemented, that senior officials accused of serious abuses should have been prosecuted, and that the Commission declined to focus sufficiently on abuses in Western Sahara. (Amnesty International, Broken Promises: The Equity and Reconciliation Commission and Its Follow-Up, January 2010.)

40 U.S. Geological Survey, "Phosphate Rock: Mineral Commodity Summary," 2014. Morocco's Royal Office of Phosphates, or OCP, has a monopoly on the mineral's extraction, processing, and commercialization.

41 CIA World Factbook, updated June 2014.

42 International Monetary Fund (IMF) World Economic Outlook database, October 2014.

43 State Department, 2014 Investment Climate Statement – Morocco, June 2014; and World Economic Forum, Global Competitiveness Report 2013-2014, "Morocco," at http://www3.weforum.org/docs/GCR2013-14/Morocco.pdf.

44 IMF, Request for an Arrangement Under the Precautionary and Liquidity Line and Cancellation of the Current Arrangement, July 11, 2014.

45 IMF, "Morocco – IMF Staff Conduct 2014 Article IV Consultations, First Review of the Precautionary and Liquidity Line," November 17, 2014.

46 Forbes.com, "King of Rock," June 17, 2009; and "The 5 Richest Kings in Africa," June 3, 2014.

47 Souhail Karam, "Morocco Regulator in Pledge on Monarchy-Owned Firms," Reuters, September 30, 2011.

48 See CRS Report RS20962, Western Sahara.

[49] State Department, Country Reports on Human Rights Practices for 2013, "Western Sahara," April 2014.

[50] In 2002, the U.N. Legal Counsel, in response to a query from the Security Council on the legality of contracts concluded by Morocco offshore Western Sahara, concluded that such activities are illegal "if conducted in disregard of the needs and interests of the people" of the "Non-Self-Governing Territory," that is, Western Sahara. This determination is not readily enforceable, but appears to have affected the calculations of private companies seeking to operate in the area. See U.N. doc. S/2002/161, Letter Dated 29 January 2002 from the Under-Secretary-General for Legal Affairs, the Legal Counsel, Addressed to the President of the Security Council, February 12, 2002.

[51] In particular, King Mohammed VI has recently increased his outreach to francophone Africa, where Morocco has longstanding diplomatic, commercial, and security interests. See Haim Malka, "Morocco's Rediscovery of Africa," Center for Strategic and International Studies, July 2013.

[52] In remarks at the U.N. General Assembly on September 25, 2014, Benkirane stated that "Western countries and their affiliated institutions, all they do is give lessons, and at best, a few pieces of advice. As for support, it is very limited and is always conditional." Transcript via Congressional Quarterly.

[53] Reuters, "Morocco Sues Activists in France over Torture Accusations," March 26, 2014; Jeune Afrique, "Salaheddine Mezouar: 'La France n'est pas engagée avec nous,'" January 9, 2015.

[54] Le Monde, "'Charlie Hebdo' absent des pays du Maghreb," January 14, 2015.

[55] Eric Schmitt, "U.S. Adds Planes to Bolster Drive to Wipe Out ISIS," New York Times, November 26, 2014.

[56] Morocco is the only country in Africa not to be a member of the AU, having withdrawn in 1984 from the AU's predecessor organization over the latter's recognition of the SADR.

[57] Morocco and U.S. officials regularly state that Morocco was the first country to recognize the United States, in 1777. The State Department Office of the Historian dates recognition to the two countries' treaty of peace and friendship in 1786 ("A Guide to the United States' History of Recognition [...] by Country, Since 1776: Morocco." See also State Department, "U.S. Relations with Morocco," Fact Sheet, August 12, 2014, which cites recognition that year).

[58] Testimony of William V. Roebuck, House Foreign Affairs Committee, April 9, 2014, op. cit.; White House, "U.S.- Morocco Strong and Enduring Commitment," Fact Sheet, November 22, 2013.

[59] The sale of F-16s has drawn particular attention in the region, where Algeria—reportedly the biggest regional arms purchaser—reportedly maintains air superiority, although U.S. officials indicated that the sale would not alter the regional balance of power. According to the Stockholm International Peace Research Institute (SIPRI), Algeria and Morocco were the world's 6th- and 12th-largest arms importers, respectively, between 2008 and 2012.

[60] Office of the U.S. Trade Representative (USTR), "Morocco," May 1, 2014.

[61] U.S. International Trade Commission statistics on U.S.-Morocco trade between 2006 and 2013, consulted January 2015. On the FTA, see CRS Report RS21464, Morocco-U.S. Free Trade Agreement, by Raymond J. Ahearn.

[62] USTR, "Morocco," op. cit.; U.S. International Trade Commission statistics, consulted January 2015.

[63] See, e.g., State Department, "Joint Statement of the Second Session of the United States - Kingdom of Morocco Strategic Dialogue," April 4, 2014. Identical language was used by

then-Secretary of State Hillary Clinton in 2011. State Department, Remarks by United States Secretary of State Hillary Rodham Clinton and Moroccan Foreign Minister Taieb Fassi Fihri, March 23, 2011, Washington, DC.

[64] Testimony of William V. Roebuck, then-Deputy Assistant Secretary of State for Near Eastern Affairs, before the House Foreign Affairs Committee, Subcommittee on the Middle East and North Africa, April 9, 2014.

[65] State Department, FY2015 Congressional Budget Justification for Foreign Operations, March 2014.

[66] USAID, USAID/Morocco Country Development Cooperation Strategy, 2013-2017.

[67] USAID, "Morocco," at http://www.usaid.gov/morocco.

[68] See MCC, "Morocco Compact," http://www.mcc.gov/pages/countries/program/morocco-compact.

[69] MCC, "MCC, Moroccan Government Announce Plans to Invest in Innovative Partnerships in Vocational Training," November 20, 2014. The announcement followed a similar statement by Vice President Joe Biden at the Global Entrepreneurship Summit in Marrakesh, Morocco.

[70] The reporting requirement was in the Senate report (S.Rept. 113-195) accompanying S. 2499 (the Senate version of the bill). The explanatory statement accompanying Division J of P.L. 113-235 indicates that "Federal departments, agencies, commissions, and other entities shall comply with the directives, reporting requirements, instructions, and allocations contained in H.Rept. 113-499 [...] and S.Rept. 113-195 [...] unless specifically directed to the contrary."

[71] Previously, the conference report on the FY2012 Consolidated Appropriations Act (P.L. 112-74, December 23, 2011) stated that, "The conferees note that funds provided in title III of this Act [bilateral economic assistance] for Morocco may be used in regions and territories administered by Morocco. The conferees remain concerned with resolving the dispute over the Western Sahara and urge the Department of State to prioritize a negotiated settlement."

[72] See footnote number 70. P.L. 112-74 (Consolidated Appropriations Act, 2012; Division I, §7041[g]) required such a report. That requirement was carried over into FY2014 via S.Rept. 113-81, accompanying S. 1372 (the Senate draft FY2014 Department of State, Foreign Operations, and Related Programs Appropriations Act).

In: Morocco
Editor: Wilson Graves

ISBN: 978-1-63485-107-7

Chapter 2

FROM ASSISTANCE TO PARTNERSHIP: MOROCCO AND ITS FOREIGN POLICY IN WEST AFRICA*

Mohammed El-Katiri

FOREWORD

Morocco is seeking to position itself as a regional security provider in West Africa. Over recent years, Morocco has emerged as a key partner for the development of variety of sectors in different West African countries, but it also aspires to contribute to peace and stability of this African sub-region that continues to face important challenges and significant threats. In particular, a range of initiatives is under way to combat religious extremism, terrorism, and transnational organized crime including illicit drug trafficking, which remains a major threat to peace and security in the region.

At a time of deepening budget constraints, bilateral cooperation with reliable and moderate regional partners offers a potential means of reducing costs while still maintaining regional reach in order to pursue U.S. security objectives. Morocco's new efforts and initiative offer synergies with U.S. priorities for the region. Morocco, with its geographic location, political stability, and close cultural ties with Sub-Saharan Africa, offers itself as a potential

* This is an edited, reformatted and augmented version of a monograph issued by the Strategic Studies Institute, November 2015.

partner to the U.S. defense community to maintain U.S. influence in the region and address shared security concerns.

In this monograph, Dr. Mohammed El-Katiri focuses on the geopolitical, security, and economic drivers of the renewed Moroccan interest in Sub-Saharan Africa. He highlights Morocco's contribution to counterextremism in West Africa and the Sahel region through initiatives promoting moderate Islam, and concludes with a number of recommendations on how Morocco could be supported by the United States in tackling some key common challenges arising from these sub-regions of Africa.

DOUGLAS C. LOVELACE, JR.
Director
Strategic Studies Institute and U.S. Army War College Press

SUMMARY

Moroccan foreign policy is currently emphasizing its presence and relations in Sub-Saharan Africa, and in particular West Africa. The wide range of cooperative projects undertaken in recent years extends to security relations, with Morocco seeking to position itself as a regional security provider.

Morocco's renewed interest in sub-Saharan Africa is driven to a large extent by the remarkable economic performance of a variety of African economies over the last decade, and the potential for continued growth over coming decades. Several African countries have been seeing much greater—and increasing—economic activity, particularly those rich in natural resources such as, but not limited to, copper, gold, oil, and gas.

But shared security has also emerged as an important aspect of Morocco's relations with a range of Sahel and West African countries. Moroccan decisionmakers see that peace and stability in the Sahel is not only a basic requirement for their own economic development but, thanks to shared security concerns, is also of prime importance to the stability of Morocco. Over the last decade, Morocco has showed intense interest in supporting peace and security in the region, through regional and broader multilateral forums such as the United Nations, the North Atlantic Treaty Organization, and the European Union.

Morocco is leveraging a range of factors—including historic ties, domestic political stability, unique economic and institutional development experience, its strategically important geographic location, and relations with

Western countries—to strengthen its position in West Africa. Morocco also aspires to position itself as a partner of choice for the United States and other organizations seeking to develop their interests in Sub-Saharan Africa. This therefore provides opportunities for the United States to leverage common interests in security and stability in the region.

INTRODUCTION

Morocco has been deepening and accelerating its engagement with Western African countries since the ascendance to the throne of the current King, Mohammed VI, in July 1999. This is evidenced by the numerous visits paid by the Moroccan King to a variety of West and Central African countries since 2000, and the number of commercial and cooperation agreements signed over the last decade. Some of the Moroccan monarch's tours lasted for weeks, signaling not only the importance that the Moroccan state gives to sub-Saharan Africa, and in particular, the West Africa region, but also indicating the King's personal fondness for these African countries.

The desire to diversify economic partners remains Morocco's main driver for strengthening and expanding its ties with West African countries. The strong economic growth achieved over the last 2 decades in a number of these states has drawn the attention of Morocco's political and economic elites to the region. Several Western African countries, such as Cote d'Ivoire, Guinea-Conakry, Sierra Leone, and Equatorial Guinea, have rich endowments of mineral resources like ores and petroleum. Their economies have benefited from the surge in international prices for commodities and the emergence of growing middle classes. Moroccan interest in Africa is also driven by the necessity to gather political support among sub-Saharan African countries for Morocco's claims to the Western Sahara territory.

Morocco leverages its political connections with a variety of Western African rulers to facilitate business opportunities for its private investors and state-owned commercial institutions. Though Morocco has not been a member of the African Union since 1984, its relations with sub-Saharan countries and involvement in the continent's security and development matters have never ceased. Morocco has long-standing and excellent relations with a number of West African countries such as Gabon, Senegal, and Cote d'Ivoire. Successive Moroccan Monarchs have persisted in efforts to maintain and establish new co-operative and productive relationships. Furthermore, unlike European and, in general, Western countries, Morocco benefits along with Western African countries from not carrying any colonial baggage. On the contrary, against the background of Morocco's own struggles for full political sovereignty from the French during the 1950s, Morocco has managed to gain a reputation among Western African political leaders as a trusted ally, proactive in addressing African development and security challenges.

Morocco's current engagement in West Africa is multifaceted; it focuses on security cooperation, economic development, strengthening cultural ties, and capacity building. Moroccan authorities consider a more comprehensive approach will be necessary; one that embraces a sustained, and long-term investment in the region's security and economic and human development.

Seen from Morocco, this comprehensive strategy entails the exchange of experiences and expertise in institutional capacity building in a variety of key sectors that are of importance to the socio-economic development of West African societies. What characterizes the current strategy is the significant involvement of the Moroccan private sector. This involvement is unlike previous cooperation and engagement efforts that were limited to ministries and publicly owned institutions.

Security assistance forms an essential component of Morocco's pivot to West African countries. Without security and stability in these African countries, Morocco cannot achieve its economic and commercial objectives, since its own security is directly affected. Moroccan officials consider these regions to be Morocco's hinterland, given their geographical proximity and strong commercial and cultural ties, but also because some of the security menaces are cross–border in nature, including the trafficking of drugs, weapons, and people.

This monograph focuses on the geopolitical and economic drivers for the renewed Morrocan interest in West Africa. It also examines how Morocco is conducting its foreign and security policy in a variety of Western African countries. It highlights Morocco's contribution to counterextremism in the West Africa and Sahel regions by training African Mosques' imams and preachers. It concludes with recommendations on how Morocco could be supported by the U.S. defense community in tackling some of the key security challenges that are facing these sub-regions of Africa for the mutual benefit of both countries. Given the common interest between the United States and Morocco in preserving peace and stability in Morocco's surrounding region, Rabat's growing assertiveness in West Africa presents an opportunity, rather than a challenge, for U.S. interests. Morocco's geographic location, political stability, and deep and long-standing cultural ties with sub-Saharan states provide a potential bridgehead for U.S. efforts to promote its security objectives in Africa. At a time of severe defense budget constraints, bilateral cooperation with reliable and moderate regional partners can provide an effective multiplier and augment the U.S. reach into otherwise challenging regions.

A History of Strong Ties with West Africa

Morocco's bilateral relations with Western African countries are not of recent origin. These relations date back centuries to the time of different ruling dynasties that governed Morocco, such as the Almoravids and Almohads, as well as the current Alawi dynasty that has ruled since 1666. These previous rulers traded with sub-Saharan African countries and maintained close social and religious links. Relations continued despite challenges posed by a variety of political events, including the French protectorate and later decolonization debates.

After independence from the French and Spanish colonial rule in 1956, Morocco continued its relations with African countries. Moroccan engagement initially was driven by a desire to help colonized countries to achieve their independence through providing support to liberation movements and supporting their cause in international circles. Morocco was a key founding member of the Organization of African Unity (OAU, now called the African Union [AU]), an organization that initially was established to support African territories and peoples to gain their freedom and independence.[1]

In the 1970s, cultivating the support of sub-Saharan African countries for Morocco's claims on Western Sahara became an important factor, one that continues to drive Moroccan foreign policy until today. Moroccan diplomacy became very active in attempts to deny the Sahrawi Arab Democratic Republic (RASD) any new recognition, and pursue African countries that had recognized RASD to withdraw their recognition. The effectiveness of Morocco's African foreign policy was evident from the failure of the Nineteenth Annual Summit of the OAU in August 1982 in Tripoli, Libya, to achieve its two-thirds quorum, after a large number of African countries supporting Morocco boycotted the summit in protest at the admission of RASD as a member of the organization.[2] The later acceptance of RASD as a member of the OAU, in turn, led Morocco to withdraw its membership in this pan-African organization, a situation which persists today.[3]

The unresolved Western Sahara issue continues to dominate Morocco's foreign policy towards African countries and the AU. In June 2014, the appointment of former Mozambican president Joaquim Chissano by the AU as a special envoy for Western Sahara revived Morocco's tensions with the organization, but also highlighted how pervasive this territorial dispute still is in Morocco's relations with African countries. Morocco objected to this appointment or any specific AU role, stressing that handling of this issue remains the exclusive domain of the United Nations (UN) Security Council and the Secretary-General.[4]

However, the withdrawal of Morocco from the AU in 1984 did not interrupt Morocco's bilateral relations with many African countries and engagement with the continent's development and security issues. Morocco has participated in many conferences and meetings concerning the African continent at UN, European Union (EU), and African levels. For example, Morocco played an active role in initiating a dialogue between African countries and the EU on migration and development in 2006, known as the Rabat Process. The main objective of this initiative was to bring together countries of origin, transit, and destination in Europe to discuss the migration phenomenon not only from a strictly security angle, but also from a development perspective.[5] Morocco initiated or joined other pan-African organizations to promote regional cooperation on a variety of issues, such as the Ministerial Conference on Fisheries Cooperation among African States Bordering the Atlantic Ocean that has its secretariat based in the Moroccan capital, Rabat; and the Community of Sahel-Sahara states (CEN-SAD) that Morocco joined in February 2001.[6]

Despite Morocco's limited financial resources and position as a major recipient of international aid for the past 30 years, the country has continued to provide humanitarian and technical assistance to African countries in order to maintain its influence and signal its solidarity and commitment to the African continent's causes. Over recent decades, Morocco has set up military hospitals and sent food and medical aid on a variety of occasions when Western African countries suffered from conflicts or natural disasters. The most recent humanitarian initiative was the setting up of a surgical field military hospital by the Moroccan armed forces in the Malian capital of Bamako, in September 2013,[7] and in Guinea-Conakry in February 2014.[8] Morocco has also supported the development of a variety of key sectors in some West African countries by sharing its knowledge and expertise. It granted scholarships to hundreds of students and provided training to cadres from these countries.

On the bilateral level, Morocco has particularly close relations with a number of West African leaders. For instance, Congo is one of its closest allies in Africa. The late King Hassan II of Morocco and the late Gabonese President Hadj Omar Bongo Ondimba forged a cordial relationship which translated into closer ties between their two countries. The Gabonese president was one of the key supporters of Morocco's sovereignty claim over Western Sahara. Both leaders jointly staged diplomatic interventions to end crises among African countries. The close relations between the two leaders continue under their successors, King Mohammed VI, and President Ali Bongo Ondimba. Equally, Morocco's relations with Equatorial Guinea have been continuously friendly since the 1970s.

Changing Opportunities in View of West Africa's Economic Growth

The past decade has witnessed a remarkable socioeconomic development trajectory in the economies of Sub-Saharan Africa. These economic achievements and their potential have gradually changed the perception of the region among the Moroccan political and business elite. Despite glaring differences in economic structures, rates of economic growth, and political stability across sub-Saharan countries, the region as a whole has realistic future economic potential. Since 2003, Sub-Saharan Africa has had average annual growth of 5 percent. This is a significant achievement particularly at a time when many developed economies are struggling to grow. According to International Monetary Fund, some Western African countries are expected to grow at 6 percent per annum.[9] These are Burkina Faso, Côte d'Ivoire, the Democratic Republic of Congo (DRC), Equatorial Guinea, and Sierra Leone. Africa's economic progress has been driven mainly by the increase of international prices for commodities, the expansion of middle class population, and urbanization. It is also these three trends that will continue to make sub-Saharan Africa one of the fastest growing regional economies over the coming decades.

Economic growth, particularly the last 15 years, has benefited from the surge in global oil and commodities prices in major oil-exporting countries such as Nigeria. Several West African countries are resource-abundant, such as Gabon, Republic of Congo, DRC, Equatorial Guinea, Cote d'Ivoire, and Sierra Leone. West Africa's natural resources are not limited to hydrocarbons, but also include other minerals such as iron ore, precious metals, and agricultural commodities. However, sub-Saharan Africa's economic progress has also been derived from other diverse sources such as tourism and manufacturing. Demographic trends and urbanization have also contributed to growth. Africa's population is rising rapidly at a time when population growth is slowing in other global regions. With a population of 924.7 million in 2014, Sub-Saharan Africa is the world's second most populous region after Asia. The population is expected to more than double by 2050 to reach about two billion. This high growth rate is driven largely by high fertility rates, on average 5.2 children per woman (compared to a world average of 2.5). Sub-Saharan Africa is also by far the most rapidly urbanizing continent. In 2014, 37 percent of the population (345.6 million people) lived in urban areas. By 2050, about 1.1 billion will be living in cities. By 2035, about half of the population will be urban.[10]

Domestic demand has constituted an important part of this growth story. Africa's middle class—including North Africa—has expanded greatly over the last 2 decades. According to a report by the African Development Bank, the middle class doubled in size between 1990 and 2010, from 157 million to 326 million.[11] This effectively includes individuals earning between US$2 to US$20 per day. The middle class is projected to continue to grow and reach 1.1 billion (42 percent of the population) by 2060. The more affluent lifestyle associated with the middle class has contributed to increased domestic consumption in many African countries.

Another driver pushing Moroccan political and economic elites to diversify the country's economic relations by strengthening ties with faster-growing countries is uncertainty over the duration of the economic crisis in Europe, and its potential ramifications for Morocco and other traditional North African trade partners in Europe. The negative impact of the economic crisis in the EU on the Moroccan economy, whose main trading partner is the EU, has already been felt in a drop in foreign investment, the return of Moroccan immigrants, and a fall in some exports.

Morocco's external economic ambitions are also a response to the realization by African leaders of the need for external assistance and foreign investment in order to achieve the economic development required to meet the rising expectations of their people. Western African governments are keen to modernize their economies by strengthening their competitiveness and economic diversity in order to make those economies more resilient to commodities price fluctuations. Moroccan political and business elites see in this expansion of public investment in West Africa, and in the rise of the middle class, a variety of business opportunities, which has encouraged them to set up production plants and distribution channels for consumer goods as well as engaging in the building of infrastructure projects. This is discernible in investment projects announced by Moroccan public and private entities over the last 5 years. A good example of this trend is the investment of the Moroccan property developer, Addoha, in building affordable housing in Mali, Congo-Brazzaville, and Cameroon; as well as cement factories in Cameroon, Cote d'Ivoire, Guinea-Conakry, Gabon, Burkina Faso, and Congo-Brazzaville.[12]

What characterizes the current Moroccan foreign policy towards sub-Saharan Africa, compared to previous engagements, is that it is a coherent and well-orchestrated strategy with a strong backing from the Moroccan palace. The dossier of rapprochement with African countries is handled at Palace level; it is in the hands of the King and his entourage. The Ministry of Foreign Affairs and other ministries play a minor role in developing this emerging relationship. Their role is limited to executing what is assigned to them and implementing the previously agreed cooperation agreement.

Morocco's current African strategy is proactive. Moroccan institutions have analyzed market potentials and gone on to pursue them. This is different from what characterized Morocco's relations with Africa under the late King Hassan II, which were mainly conducted on an ad hoc basis with the single goal of securing African states' diplomatic support on the Western Sahara issue. However, this does not argue that the current rapprochement does not achieve such diplomatic influence. It certainly does, but also in full alignment with other socio-economic and security objectives.

The formulation of Morocco's grand strategy towards Africa has been based, to a large extent, on the investment experience of the country's financial institutions in French-speaking Africa. Morocco's three leading banks—Attijariwafa Bank, Banque marocaine du commerce extérieur (BMCE), and Banque Centrale Populaire (BCP)—have boosted their retail banking presence in several sub-Saharan African countries since 2005. Moroccan lenders are now occupying leading positions within the African banking landscape in terms of assets and regional network coverage.[13] Attijariwafa bank has 414 branches in 11 West and Central African countries.[14] BCP, after taking control of the Ivorian Banque Atlantique in 2012 to add to its earlier acquisitions of Banque populaire Morocco-Centrafricaine and Banque populaire Marocco-Guineenne, has a presence in seven countries of the West African Economic and Monetary Union. BMCE Bank with its 72.6 percent stake in Bank of Africa has an extensive geographical coverage. In 2014, BMCE was present in 16 countries with a total of 461 branches.[15] BMCE is the only Moroccan bank that operates not only in French-speaking Africa, but also has a presence and a plan to expand into English-speaking African countries in Central and East Africa.

The remarkable experience of Moroccan banks' expansion in Western and Central African countries has inspired other Moroccan companies to seek opportunities in a variety of sectors. The systematic insights and contacts that such institutions have aggregated from these African countries have contributed to the formulation of the new Moroccan foreign policy towards sub-Saharan Africa. The dominance of economic elements in Morocco's ongoing engagement with sub-Saharan African countries, and the nature of investment and economic partnership agreements inked so far, are an indication of the contribution of Morocco's early banking investments. Those charged with the formulation of Moroccan policy and strategy towards sub-Saharan Africa have benefited from detailed insights on business opportunities in these African countries.

What is different now? Morocco has aggregated immense expertise in a variety of fields that are needed for the development of African countries. Morocco, during the 15 years rule of King Mohammed VI, has launched major economic, social, and security projects that have given Moroccan private and public institutions significant experience and relevant skill sets. Moroccan companies in variety of sectors—from banking, agriculture, real estate, and pharmaceutical to physical infrastructure development—have accumulated extensive industry knowledge, experience, and financial wealth that allow them to expand internationally.

A few leading Moroccan conglomerates, such as Addoha, Cooper Pharma Maroc, and the National Office of Electricity, have made accessing sub-Saharan African markets an important part of their internationalization strategies. Several of these companies have inked contracts to build overseas manufacturing units during the last 3 years.

The expansion of the Moroccan state-owned *Office Chérien des Phosphates* (OCP) into Africa exemplifies Morocco's new economic strategy towards Africa. With its rising population and agriculture production potential, sub-Saharan Africa is increasingly becoming an important growth market for the OCP, a world leading phosphate fertilizers producer.

OCP has set up a new production unit in Jarf Las-far, a Moroccan industrial park and port south of Casablanca that exports its entire production to Sub-Saharan Africa. OCP has even developed specific fertilizing products that are suitable for West Africa soils, such as the Teractive fertilizer that is designed for local crops, including: cotton, cocoa, and corn. Ivory Coast is by far the largest cocoa producer in the world followed by Ghana. Adding Nigeria and Cameroon, the combined share is around 70 percent of global production.[16]

In March 2014, OCP and Gabon's state-owned mining company, Société Équatoriale des Mines, signed a partnership agreement to develop a fertilizer manufacturing industry involving both countries and dedicated entirely to meeting demand in Sub-Saharan Africa. The logic behind this joint venture is to exploit synergies between the phosphate and natural gas resources of both countries. The partnership agreement stipulates building an ammonia plant in Gabon that uses natural gas feedstock, and a phosphate fertilizers production unit. Morocco undertakes to build two phosphoric acid facilities and a unit to produce phosphate-based fertilizers in Morocco. OCP's partnership with Gabon is driven both by the desire to tap into new growing markets in Sub-Saharan Africa, and by a need to access natural gas resources that constitute an important input to produce fertilizers. This project symbolizes the kind of partnerships by Moroccan private and public institutions that are willing to pursue the creation of wealth and achieve economic development across the continent.

GATEWAY TO AFRICA

The strengthening of the presence of Moroccan companies in sub-Saharan Africa is one pillar of Morocco's new economic strategy. A second pillar focuses on positioning Morocco as both a hub and foothold for international companies with an interest in expanding across the African continent. BMCE bank was the first Moroccan bank to see an opportunity in becoming a hub for Africa by capitalizing on Morocco's linguistic, political, and cultural connections with a number of African countries. In 2007, BMCE set up an investment bank in London (MediCapital Bank, since 2010 renamed BMCE Bank International Plc), with a business mandate to harness international partnership opportunities with interest in sub-Sahara Africa, particularly French-speaking Africa.[17] Leveraging its expertise and experience in working in sub-Saharan Africa, BMCE has hoped to encourage international investment into Africa and Morocco itself. Though BMCE's experience in London was not a great success, the idea of Morocco serving as a gateway for international investors to expand into to North and West-African countries was adopted by Moroccan decisionmakers, and the launch of the Casablanca Financial City project in 2010 reflects this adoption.

Casablanca Financial City is meant to become a financial hub for the French-speaking African market. Many of the major multinational manufacturers that have set up production units in Morocco have been attracted by the possibilities of accessing African markets. The most recent example is the decision by the French-based automaker, PSA Peugeot Citroën, to build a manufacturing facility in Morocco, with plans to produce 200,000 cars and 200,000 motorcycles annually. One of the main factors driving this investment, in addition to the availability of affordable skilled labor, is the potential for accessing sub-Saharan and Middle-Eastern markets[18] by taking advantage of Morocco's network of free trade agreements and excellent political ties across these two regions.

Solidarity and Crisis Management Help

Morocco's reconnection with West Africa is not limited only to business contracts and official visits; many of Morocco's economic initiatives over the last few years have been launched with an important social dimension in mind. Over the last 3 years in particular, Morocco has adopted several initiatives to show solidarity with Western African countries.

In 2014, Morocco launched its first program to legalize immigrants from a variety of African countries who had lived in Morocco for years, waiting for an opportunity to immigrate to Europe. The change of official attitude in Morocco towards illegal immigrants is not driven by the need for workers, as used to be the case in many European countries up until a few years ago. Morocco is a country with a young population that is larger than the current economy can provide with adequate job opportunities. Nor is Morocco prosperous enough to provide thousands of immigrants with basic socio-economic services such as education and heath care.

Morocco's tolerance of African illegal immigration has two other explanations. First, this is an attempt by the Moroccan government to refute media reporting alleging racist and inhumane treatment of illegal African immigrants. Second, this tolerance is an attempt to show Morocco's solidarity with other African peoples: this is a move to win the hearts and minds of Africans and demonstrate a difference from the approaches adopted by many European countries.

Morocco showed its solidarity again during the 2014 Ebola outbreak in West Africa, which is considered to be one of the most severe, prolonged, and complicated outbreaks to have affected the region in decades, with 22,859 infection cases and a total of 9,162 deaths, according to statistics published in February 2015.[19] When most international air carriers were suspending their flights to Western African airports over fear of virus contagion, Morocco's air carrier, Royal Air Maroc (RAM), continued flights, including to the areas most affected by the Ebola epidemic; Sierra Leone, Liberia, and Guinea.[20] The continuation of RAM flights in and out of Western African airports allowed international medical aid workers to arrive at the affected areas, and Western African citizens to stay connected with the world. Maintaining scheduled flights was also a clear message of solidarity with Western African countries.

This gesture was well-received by the political leadership in Western African capitals. During the High-Level International Conference on Ebola organized in Brussels in March 2015, Alpha Conde, the president of Guinea, praised Morocco's stance for keeping its borders open, allowing the free movement of people.[21] These initiatives are designed in senior Moroccan political circles to boost the country's status as a reliable ally and partner for African countries. The strategy appears to be bearing fruit. The Moroccan monarch seems to have won the sympathy of West African societies and leaders, as indicated by the number of popular receptions given to the King during his June tour of Senegal, Guinea-Bissau, Côte d'Ivoire, and Gabon.[22]

Security Cooperation

Morocco has now, more than ever, vested interests in seeing Sub-Saharan Africa, and West Africa in particular, politically stable, secure, and prosperous. Increased Moroccan economic presence in West African economies will posit an important Moroccan role in the security of the region. In the event of political instability and chaos, it is Morocco which would suffer most directly, being West Africa's main gateway for illegal trafficking into Europe. Having fought a long-standing, and so far relatively successful, battle against both Arab Spring-style popular protest movements on the one hand, and radical Islamist terrorism on the other, Morocco has a strong incentive to prevent the creation of political flash points near its hard to control southern borders, or of safe havens for international terrorist cells, whether religious in nature or not. Furthermore, substantial Moroccan investment projects include manufacturing plants and infrastructure projects that require stability to continue production. Prolonged disruptions of business operations due to any political or social instability would adversely affect these Moroccan investments. Without security and stability in these African countries, Morocco cannot achieve its economic and commercial objectives.

For example, the political and military crisis in Cote d'Ivoire that began in 2002, and particularly the serious post-election crisis that followed the announcement of the results of the second round of the presidential election on November 28, 2010, resulted in large-scale economic disruption that adversely impacted Moroccan investment and diaspora remittances.[23] Attijariwafa Bank, through its subsidiary the Ivorian Society Bank, incurred a drop in its revenues, as it had to close down its operations for months during the height of the 2011 crisis.[24] Banque populaire Morocco-Centrafricaine is another Moroccan-owned financial institution that has been adversely affected by deep political, security, and economic crises in Central African Republic.[25] The economic disruptions as a result of this conflict negatively impacted the bank's performance.[26] For the Moroccan ruling circle, this is also a matter that affects personal wealth since many of its members hold shares, board memberships, and commercial roles in these companies.

Although the worst political and criminal violence across the region appears to be over, the security situation across West Africa, as is the case in several other sub-Saharan regions, remains particularly volatile. Decades of political turmoil and armed conflicts have left the region's state authorities weak and unable to control nonstate armed groups or the illicit traffic of drugs and people in their respective territories, or to set up an effective regional security force.[27] Since 2011, the flood of weapons from the Libyan conflict has also added to insecurity throughout West Africa, as rebels, terrorist groups, and criminal organizations benefit from the movement of arms and fighters. The rapid economic growth experienced in some countries has not benefited all citizens and provinces evenly. This fragile security and political situations has undoubtedly been a serious challenge to West African governments and their international partners.

Morocco's concerns about security challenges in West Africa preceded its renewed economic interest in this African sub-region. Given their international nature, the rise of terrorism, piracy and armed robbery at sea in the Gulf of Guinea, and illicit trafficking of drugs and humans in West African countries have always been perceived as direct threats to Morocco. Given Morocco's geographic location, criminal groups based in West Africa are tempted to use Moroccan territory as a transit point to smuggle migrants, cocaine, or other narcotics to Europe. In fact, Morocco has become a major transit hub for the trafficking of migrants. Also, over the last decade, there have been many stories in the Moroccan press about seizures of cocaine proceeding from West African countries through Moroccan ports and airports.[28] In particular, the nexus between organized crime and terrorism remains the most alarming to Moroccan security authorities. There is concern about the use of financial proceeds from drug and human trafficking by terrorist organizations within Morocco or at its borders to carry out systematic attacks within the country.

Against this background, it is not surprising that Morocco has shown interest in playing an important role in helping West Africa and Sahel countries tackle their significant and complex security challenges over the last decade, and particularly after the events of the Arab Spring in 2011. Moroccan diplomacy has been continuously active and supportive of a variety of initiatives and debates in African, European, and UN forums, calling for structural solutions to West Africa and Sahel security problems. For instance, King Mohammed VI, in a speech addressed to the 69th session of the UN General Assembly, called on developed countries to change their attitude towards African development matters and treat African countries with fairness and objectivity. He asserted that "Africa does not need humanitarian aid as much as it needs mutually beneficial partnerships."[29]

Moroccan officials argue that their engagement in support of peace and stability in West Africa is not a novelty. Morocco's armed forces have participated in numerous peace missions in Africa since independence in 1956, and have provided military assistance to West African nations either under the umbrella of the UN or bilaterally to its allies since the 1960s. For instance, Morocco contributed to the stability of Zaire (now the DRC) in 1977 by sending a large Moroccan military contingent. The mission of Moroccan troops, leading a pan-African force, was to assist President Mobutu Sese Seko to restore control and stability in Shaba, a mineral-rich province, after the withdrawal of a Franco-Belgian force which had repulsed attacks by an Angola-based rebel group.[30] Another Western African country that benefited from Moroccan military assistance is Equatorial Guinea. In September 1979, Morocco sent 100 military officers to the then newly appointed President Teodoro Obiang Nguema, after a military coup that deposed Francisco Macias Nguema on August 3, 1979.[31] Morocco maintained its security assistance to Teodoro Obiang Nguema, who still rules Equatorial Guinea today. Morocco has also contributed to UN peacekeeping forces in several West African countries including the Congo in 1960, the DRC in 1999 and in Côte d'Ivoire in 2004.[32] Furthermore, Morocco has offered hundreds of military officers from West African armies opportunities to receive education and training in Moroccan military academies alongside Moroccan officers.

Since 2012, Morocco has assumed a more assertive role in its foreign policy towards the West Africa and Sahel regions. The changes and challenges brought by the Arab spring in North Africa have created a new geopolitical environment for Morocco. The killing of Libyan leader Muammar Qadhafi in

2011 gave Morocco an opportunity to play an active role in one of the already existing pan-African economic and security cooperation organizations and initiatives. During his rule, Qadhafi had had an assertive foreign policy in the Sahel and other parts of Africa, using Libya's financial resources and his unity ideology to gain influence.[33] Morocco's foreign policy attitude at that time was to avoid any competition and potential confrontation with Qadhafi for a leadership role in these African regions, and to opt instead for a more subtle approach working on a bilateral basis with West African countries.

Another significant change in North Africa's geopolitical environment is the perception in Rabat and in Western capitals of Algeria's shift away from playing an active role in the Sahel. The rapid deterioration of security environment along almost all Algerian borders in addition to the country's acute internal social problems have forced the Algerian leadership to take a defensive position, and show little interest in playing a major role in the security of the region. Algeria's refusal to participate in any Western-led military intervention in northern Mali, and its preference for a diplomatic solution has been widely interpreted as a withdrawal from the Sahel.[34] It is beyond the scope of this monograph to discuss in details the motives of Algerian stances on the Libya and Mali security situations, but this is interpreted as a tactical retreat, allowing Algerian military strategists to adapt to the new complex geopolitical scene next to their borders. Algerian political and military elites have resisted being drawn into any exhausting war in the region with little prospect of resolution but have, similarly to Morocco, been affected negatively by the trafficking of weapons, people, and radical ideas pushing through its southern and eastern frontiers.

In this context, the Moroccan authorities saw an opportunity to expand Morocco's influence and assume a hegemonic role in the region. Morocco organized a series of conferences and meetings to discuss ways and means to fight transnational organized crime and terrorism, including illicit drug trafficking, which remains a major threat to peace and security in the Sahel and West Africa regions. In November 2013, Morocco held the Second Regional Ministerial Conference on border security between Sahel and Maghreb States that brought senior officials from the region together with representatives from the United States, France, and EU. Morocco offered to host the headquarters of a regional border security management training center that was agreed at the conference.[35]

The establishment of this center was a response to an acute security problem that affects many countries in the region. Many governments are unable or unwilling to exercise full control of their own borders, or coordinate with their neighboring countries on joint surveillance operations, a weakness that is exploited by terrorists and traffickers. Terrorists in particular find it straightforward to carry out attack operations and then flee to another country, seeking sanctuary. Once established, the center will provide training to officers with responsibility for border security management in the states of the region, as well as allow for sharing of expertise and best practices—in terms of institutions, policies, laws and procedures—from other leading international partners.

Since early-2012, Morocco has been leading efforts to revive and restructure the Community of Sahel-Saharan States (CEN-SAD), an intergovernmental organization with 28 members that was closely associated with the late Libyan ruler, Qadhafi.[36] Morocco advocates the need for strengthening CEN-SAD in order to tackle the region's precarious security situation. Since a January 2012 meeting in Addis Ababa, Ethiopia, Morocco has hosted several meetings to discuss the issue of reorganizing the organization to tackle security challenges through a comprehensive approach placed at the center of each meeting agenda. The drive to reshape the organization and allow it to build a collective security mechanism is a response to the failures and inability of Sahel and West African countries to coordinate responses to recent crises in Mali, Guinea-Bissau, and Central African Republic; as well as their inability to enhance border controls and fight terrorism.

Morocco appears to allocate great importance to these meetings and efforts, as is evident from the involvement and support of the highest decisionmaking figures within Morocco. For instance, during the October 2013 CEN-SAD meeting in Rabat, Moroccan Foreign Minister Salaheddine Mezouar highlighted the importance of amending the policies of the Sahelo-Saharian Investment and Commerce Bank, a subsidiary organ of CEN-SAD, to allow it to play a bigger role in the socio-economic development of its member countries.[37]

Morocco's hegemonic ambitions in the Maghreb and Sahel regions also remain a driving force behind its active role in strengthening and playing a leading role in CEN-SAD. A strong organization with efficient political and economic organs, and clear security objectives will undermine Algeria's main security initiative in the Sahel, *Comité d'état-major opérationnel conjoint* (CEMOC). CEMOC was launched by Algeria in April 2010 with the aim of coordinating counterterrorism efforts and conducting joint patrols and cross-border operations between Algerian, Nigerien, Mauritanian, and Malian forces.[38]

COUNTERTERRORISM THROUGH THE TRAINING OF RELIGIOUS PREACHERS

Perhaps the most visible indication of Morocco's distinctive influence in West Africa and Sahel regions is its contribution to counterterrorism, primarily through counterextremism, by training religious personnel in the Moroccan experience of reforming religious affairs. In recent years, there has been growing interest in receiving Moroccan assistance in this field from West Africa and Sahel countries. During King Mohammed VI's visit to Mali in September 2013, the Moroccan Ministry of Endowments and Islamic Affairs agreed to provide training to 500 Malian imams. The purpose of this 2-year training is to ensure that religious leaders preach moderate messages to the public, and that they are prepared to engage in theological debates to challenge extremist views.[39]

Other countries, such as Guinea-Conakry, Cote d'Ivoire, Nigeria, Tunisia, and Libya have approached Morocco for the same training for their Imams and preachers in order to benefit from Moroccan experience in tackling extremism through dialogue and communication. To respond to the surge in demand for training of religious personnel, Morocco established the Mohammed VI Institute for the Training of Imams, Morchidines, and Morchidates (female Islamic preachers) in March 2015, with capacity to train up to 1,000 candidates.[40] A few months later, in July 2015, the Moroccan King inaugurated another pan-African religious institution, the Mohammed VI Foundation for African Ulama (Muslim religious scholars).[41] According to Royal Decree (Dahir) No.1.15.75, from its headquarters in Rabat, the foundation aims to coordinate African Muslim scholars' efforts to generate and disseminate ideas of tolerance on the basis of Islamic values, revitalize the common Islamic cultural heritage, undertake scientific research in Islamic studies, and organize events.[42] Though the foundation's competencies do not include issuance of fatwas, this initiative is likely to further strengthen Moroccan influence across Muslim communities in Africa.

Morocco's successful reform of religious affairs initiated after the 2003 Casablanca terrorist attacks has positioned the country as a leading example in the Muslim world by subtly but determinedly counteracting religious radicalism and terrorism. The reshaping of religious institutions and affairs has constituted an important part of the Moroccan government strategy to combat terrorism.[43] It is arguably not only one of the most comprehensive reform packages of religion and religious institutions in Morocco, but also in the Muslim world.

Some of the principal aspects of this reform include:

- Training and educating religious personnel, including not only those who lead worship (known as Imams), but also male and female preachers (known as Murchidin and Murchidat).
- The launch of television and radio stations whose sole purpose is to counterbalance the influence of hardline preachers, and the influence of religious satellite channels from the Middle East and Iran that spread radical Islam or Shi'ism. The ultimate aim is to achieve a high level of religious homogeneity among Moroccan Muslims and avoid the emergence of any sectarian divide in the country.
- The stipulation that only qualified scholars approved by the Moroccan Ministry of Endowments and Islamic Affairs are allowed to issue fatwas (religious legal opinion), thus preventing the involvement of unauthorized scholars and radical preachers. The only institutions authorized to issue fatwas are the High Council of Ulama (religious scholars) and Regional Ulama Councils.[44]

A further important factor that has led to official requests for Morocco's assistance in religious affairs from Western African governments is backing from important religious groups in societies that have maintained strong religious ties with Morocco. Moroccan *Sufi* orders have many followers in a range of African countries, and maintain strong ties with West African *Sufi* orders that date back centuries.

In being perceived to be moderate and flexible in terms of the diversity and nature of sources available to the Ulama to practice *Ijtihad*—reinterpreting the principles of Islam to provide legal answers to contemporary issues facing Muslims and Muslim societies—the *Maliki madhab* (Islamic legal school) that is officially adopted by Morocco aims to provide answers to contemporary issues that have not been dealt with in the fundamental texts (the *Qura'an* and *Sunnah*—Prophet Muhammad's known sayings and deeds). The *Maliki madhab* is praised for consulting more sources than the other remaining three Sunni Schools. More importantly, it accommodates local traditions and reconciles them with the teachings of fundamental texts.

Cooperation with Regional and International Partners

Despite willingness to contribute to the promotion of peace and security in the region, Moroccan officials in Rabat are aware of their own limitations. There is a recognition that the security needs of West Africa are multiple and complex, and beyond the technical, human, and financial capabilities of Morocco acting alone. The proliferation of militant groups in the region, many of which have ties to al-Qaeda in the Maghreb (AQIM) or other international terrorist organizations, remains a main challenge facing the region. It is one which requires well-trained and equipped armed forces, not only in one country but across the Sahel and West Africa region, given the transborder nature of the threats. For example, Boko Haram is a major threat for all of western Africa with proven links to AQIM and other terrorist organizations.[45] The existing military capabilities, with minimal communication networks and limited manpower resources, are not suited for effective surveillance and control over vast terrains on the edge of the Sahara desert. Furthermore, many West African militaries are not structured and trained to face the challenges with which their countries have been presented in recent years.

Morocco recognizes that it is effectively impossible for individual countries to tackle today's international security challenges on their own, and therefore acknowledges the necessity of working with regional and international partners to be able to deal systematically with cross-border security challenges. Cooperation will allow also pooling of knowledge, expertise and resources to tackle some of these security menaces that are destabilizing West Africa.

The reform of armed forces in West African countries will entail a considerable training effort in order to enable these militaries to play a more effective role in meeting current and future security challenges facing their own societies and states. As a result, security sector reform is becoming a priority policy area in order to maintain stability and achieve economic growth across the West Africa region. West Africa's armed forces and security agencies have been debilitated or deprived of opportunities to professionalize, including by decades of instability as a result of frequent regime changes and coups, which have precipitated frequent rearranging of security policies and institutions.

Morocco could play an important role with other international partners in delivering military assistance to West African countries. Morocco can leverage its linguistic access, and its understanding of military cultures, its political ties, and growing economic presence to become a hub for international donors and nongovernmental organizations that are interested in professionalizing armed forces and providing security sector reform assistance to West African countries. Strengthening the security sector requires understanding how local institutions function and building relationships with key local stakeholders, including civil society actors. With these factors in mind, Morocco is well-positioned with partnership and support from leading international associates to provide tailored training and capacity building assistance that meet the specific needs of each individual armed force across the region.

CONCLUSION

Deepening the engagement with Sub-Saharan Africa, particularly with West African countries, is what distinguishes Morocco's foreign policy under the rule of the current King, Mohammed VI. West African economies and markets are increasingly gaining importance in Morocco's ambition to diversify its export markets and seek new sources of growth for its companies. Over the last decade, sub-Saharan Africa, including West Africa, has emerged as one of the world's fastest growing regional economies. This growth momentum looks set to be maintained in the coming years.

Morocco is keen to leverage its linguistic, political, and cultural ties with West African societies and leaders in order to seek new economic development opportunities. This can be seen from the number of bilateral agreements signed during numerous visits by the Moroccan monarch to African countries, and initiatives launched in Morocco over the last few years.

Though one could argue that there is nothing new in signing training, commercial, and sectorial cooperation agreements between Morocco and sub-Saharan African countries (as there have been many such agreements signed since the 1970s and 1980s), what distinguishes Morocco's current engagement in Western Africa is the substantial involvement of private investors in a variety of sectors and countries across the continent. The experience and expertise gained by Morocco public and private sector investors over the last 15 years in a variety of fields have positioned the country as a model of socio-economic development and a desired partner for many sub-Saharan countries.

Morocco has a vital interest in preventing the deterioration of West Africa's security. It is well understood in Moroccan political circles that harnessing economic growth opportunities in Western Africa cannot be achieved without peace and security. Despite some progress in political and economic stability over recent years, the security situation remains particularly volatile, given the weak state of security institutions and the existence of large number of armed groups that are competing with some West African states for control of resources.

An important Moroccan contribution to the security of West Africa and the Sahel is in the realm of fighting religious extremism, through the sharing of the country's expertise and experience gained from the implementation of multifaceted reform of religious affairs, particularly the training and education of clerics. Morocco perceives the training of imams as an approach to preventing and countering radicalization. Fostering moderate imams will contribute to the resilience of individuals and communities against the appeal of violent extremism.

But there is appetite in Rabat to play a greater role in facilitating comprehensive solutions to West Africa security problems in cooperation with African and Sahel countries as well as with other international allies. To increase its influence, Morocco plays an increasingly active role in regional institutions, including CENSAD, particularly contributing to ongoing efforts to revitalize the role of this pan-African organization's mission, and orient its mission towards cooperation on tackling regional security problems.

Morocco's renewed interest in contributing to the security of the West Africa region, primarily through capability-building, is opening new opportunities for cooperation beyond the region to include other international partners with similar policy objectives. It also suggests new opportunities for the United States and Morocco to further strengthen their bilateral strategic dialogue by collaborating on regional matters.

IMPLICATIONS AND RECOMMENDATIONS

Morocco's new policy of engagement is an important factor in the evolving security and counterterrorism dynamic in the region. The emergence of a relatively powerful new player in security provision in Africa is a matter of immediate relevance to the U.S. Africa Command (AFRICOM), to the U.S. Army more broadly, and to the U.S. Department of State (DoS). Following and understanding the developing regional power balance in West Africa, and the redrawing of new alliances within the region, are vital not only to fostering regional security, but also to an under- standing of developments in the continent overall.

Morocco's clear incentive to enhance its own national security by acting as a regional security provider offers substantial opportunities for cooperation. Several of the problems facing Morocco lie at the root of security challenges confronting close U.S. allies in Europe: resolution of those problems calls for stronger cooperation at the state level, both in the subregion and internationally. Regional and international threats emanating from West Africa and Sahel cannot be tackled effectively without pursuing innovative partnerships and better exploitation of synergies offered by different countries. Thus, with appropriate support, Morocco's niche capabilities can be exploited to deliver professionalization programs for West African militaries, as well as other security sector reform initiatives aimed at reducing the incidence of uncontrolled migration, terrorism, trafficking in narcotics and humans, and other cross-border challenges.

This potential for collaboration has already been partially recognized, by initiatives which can now be built on. In 2004, Morocco was designated a "major non-NATO [North Atlantic Treaty Organization] U.S. ally" by President George W. Bush, as a response to the country's support and cooperation in the war on terror.[46] In practical terms, this status has allowed the Moroccan security community to benefit from U.S. military assistance and intelligence cooperation. Morocco hosts a yearly joint military exercise, Africa Lion, the largest U.S. exercise on the African continent, intended to enhance interoperability and mutual understanding. In addition, several hundred Moroccan officers have benefited from International Military Education and Training, a program funded by the DoS to enable foreign officers to attend military education at U.S. establishments.[47]

Further vectors for cooperation are provided by Morocco's relatively close relationship with NATO, as a founding member of Mediterranean Dialogue in 1994. Morocco's NATO partnership framework was renewed in 2013, with a focus on counterterrorism and interoperability.[48] This is augmented by Moroccan participation in NATO operations, and ongoing exercises and cooperation between NATO and Moroccan naval forces including U.S. Navy vessels.[49]

With its unique mix of geographical location, cultural, religious and linguistic ties, Morocco could become the international partner of choice for the U.S. defense and development communities to facilitate and jointly provide security assistance programs.

Morocco can capitalize on the same assets that have been used for its investment strategies towards Africa in order to tailor and deliver effective security assistance and security sector reforms. Moroccan military personnel and institutions are familiar with West African military officers and cultures.

Morocco has sent several military contingents and provided military education and training to hundreds of West African officers. Morocco's political stability and the professionalism of its military institutions are advantageous, both for cooperation with U.S. counterparts and for effective delivery of security assistance to recipient countries.

Morocco's long-term and continuing political stability is a further significant factor that should encourage the United States to strengthen its security cooperation and collaboration with Rabat. In a region that has experienced sustained political turmoil, Morocco today remains one of the few continuously stable countries in the Middle East and North Africa. Instead, the country's leadership has been adept in negotiating and resolving political and economic challenges. If this trend continues, it removes a number of the risks and challenges inherent in closer security relationships with Middle Eastern and North African states.

Morocco's ongoing Western Sahara territorial dispute in particular does not pose a challenge to the stability of the country, or to its external relationships. Morocco continues to favor a political settlement of the dispute, and eschews use of military force. As a result, the existence of the dispute has not prevented Morocco from developing close security cooperation with a variety of European countries, including Spain, the former colonial power in Western Sahara.

The Morocco-based training center for border security in Sahel and West Africa should be supported and enhanced. The U.S. Department of Defense (DoD) should not limit its support to establishing the training center for border security officers from West Africa and Sahel agreed in Rabat in November 2013, but it also should encourage the extension of these activities. The Center could provide a wide range of other training courses that can contribute to building the military and security capabilities of West African armed forces. Several counterterrorism training programs offered by AFRICOM through the Trans Saharan Counterterrorism Partnership could be delivered through this center, and thus benefit from funding assistance offered by the Counterterrorism Partnerships Fund. This regional training center could serve as a specialized think tank to support needs assessments undertaken by member countries, as well as providing strategic advice and guidance.

Morocco's extension of its counter-radicalism strategy to sub-Saharan Africa should be supported and encouraged. The U.S. defense community and DoS should support at arm's length Morocco's efforts to counter violent extremism through the training of religious personnel and institutionalising of religious affairs in West Africa and Sahel countries. The Moroccan experience of religious affairs reform, with proven success in counter-radicalization, should be studied closely. Lessons learned could be of help in providing similar solutions in other areas where the United States is involved in stabilization and counterterrorism operations, as well as for counter-radicalization efforts domestically and within the United States and its allies. In particular, there are substantial synergies between Morocco's counterextremism experience and expertise, and U.S. Government strategic communications initiatives across broad parts of the Muslim world; these synergies should be leveraged and exploited.

End Notes

1 Organization of African Unity, "Resolution Adopted by the First Conference of Independent African Heads of State and Government Held in Addis Ababa, Ethiopia, from 22 to 25 May 1963," CIAS/PLEN.2/REV.2, Addis Ababa, Ethiopia: Organization of African Unity, available from *www.au.int/en/sites/default/files/ ASSEMBLY_EN_22_25_MAY_1963_ ASSEMBLY_HEADS_ STATE_GOVERNMENT_FIRST_ORDINARY_SESSION.pdf.*

2 Jay Post, "Rifts Over Qadhafi, Sahara Jeopardize the Unity of Africa," *The Washington Post*, August 11, 1982, available from *www.washingtonpost.com/archive/politics/1982/08/11/ rifts-over-qaddafi-sahara-jeopardize-the-unity-of-africa/0e0818b6-d9ee-4d64-bc3c-0cd678907f93/.*

3 Morocco is the only African country that is not a member of the African Union. Morocco's decision to end its membership in the African Union (called then Organization of African Unity) came as response to the admission of a delegation claiming to represent an independent state in Western Sahara, the Sahrawi Arab Democratic Republic in 1982. For further information, see Clifford D. May, "Morocco Quits O.A.U Over Polisario," *The New York Times*, November 13, 1984, available from *www.nytimes. com/1984/11/13/world/ morocco-quits-oau-over-polisario.html.*

4 "PSC scaling up efforts to resolve the crisis in Western Sahara," Peace and Security Council Report, Pretoria, South Africa: Institute for Security Studies, April 10, 2015, available from *www. issafrica.org/pscreport/addis-insights/psc-scaling-up-efforts-to-resolvethe-crisis-in-western-sahara.*

5 Michael Collyer, "Euro-African Relations in the Field of Migration, 2008," *Panorama: The Mediterranean Year*, Barcelona, Spain: The European Institute of the Mediterranean, 2009, available from *www.iemed.org/anuari/2009/aarticles/a281.pdf.*

6 Pan-African News Agency, "Moroccan Prime Minister to attend CEN SAD summit," Pan-African News Agency, March 4, 2002, available from *www.panapress.com/Moroccan-Prime-Ministerto-attend-CEN-SAD-summit--13-455383-18-lang2-index.html.*

7 "HM the king, accompanied by Malian president, visits Moroccan field hospital in Bamako," Maghreb Arab Press, September 20, 2013, available from *www.mapnews.ma/en/activites-royales/hm-king-accompanied-malian-president-visits-moroccan-field-hospital-bamako.*

8 Nouhou Baldé, "Coopération Guinée-Maroc: encore deux semaines pour l'hôpital marocain à Conakry," ("Guinea-Morocco Cooperation: another two weeks for the Moroccan hospital in

Conakry"), *Guinee News*, May 14, 2014, available from *guineenews. org/cooperation-guinee-maroc-encore-deux-semaines-pour-lhopital- marocain-a-conakry/.*

[9] African Development Bank Group, "Tracking Africa's Progress in Figures," Tunisia: African Development Bank, 2014, available from *www.afdb-org.jp/file/news-and-pressrelease/Tracking_ Africafs_Progress_in_Figures-3.pdf.* For further information, see International Monetary Fund Reports, "Regional Economic Outlook: sub-Sahara Africa," over period from 2003 to 2014, Bretton Woods, NH: International Monetary Fund, available from *www. imf.org/external/pubs/ft/reo/2014/afr/eng/sreo1014.htm.*

[10] "World Urbanization Prospects: The 2014 Revision," New York: United Nations, Department Economic and Social Affairs, 2014, available from *esa.un.org/unpd/wup/Final Report/WUP2014- Report.pdf.*

[11] Africa Development Bank, "The Middle of the Pyramid: Dynamics of the Middle Class in Africa," *Market Brief*, April 20, 2011, available from *www.afdb.org/fileadmin/ uploads/afdb/Documents/Publications/The%20Middle%20of%20the%20Pyramid_ The%20Middle%20of%20the%20Pyramid.pdf.*

[12] Amin Rbob, "Addoha investit le logement social à Bamako," ("Addoha Invests in affordabale Housing in Bamako"), *L' Economiste*, Edition No. 4219, February 24, 2014, available from *www.leconomiste.com/article/917169-addoha-investit-le-logement-social-bamako#sthash. 0eSKLyTM.dpuf.*

[13] "Pan-African Banks: Opportunities and Challenges for Cross-Border Oversight," IMF Policy Papers, Bretton Woods, NH: International Monetary Fund, December 18, 2014, available from *www.imf.org/external/np/pp/eng/2014/121814.pdf.*

[14] "Report," Casablanca, Morocco: Attijariwafa Bank, February 2015, available from *www.attijariwafabank.com/ESPACEFINANCIER/Documents/1_AB_PLAQUETTE_DG-Dec.%202014-V. Angl.pdf.*

[15] "Annual Report 2014," Casablanca, Morocco: BMCE Bank, 2014, available from *www.bmcebank.ma/UploadFiles/publications/2180/V000002/Web%20RAPPORT%20 ABREGE%20ANG%20 XG.pdf.*

[16] "Middle Africa Cocoa Outlook: 2015, Ecobank Research, Lomé, Togo: Ecobank, February 26, 2015, available from *www.ecobank.com/upload/2015030309195944089MuBJ5zzSFJ.pdf.*

[17] "Annual Report 2012," Casablanca, Morocco: BMCE Bank, 2012, available from *www.bmcebank.ma/UploadFiles/publications/2023/V000003/RA%20P1%20 BMCE%20ANG.pdf.*

[18] Mehdi Michbal, "Automobile: tout savoir sur l'usine marocaine de PSA Peugeot Citroën," ("Automotive: everything about the Moroccan factory of PSA Peugeot Citroën"), *Jeune Afrique*, June 21, 2015, available from *www.jeuneafrique.com/238250/ economie/automobile-tout-savoir-sur-lusine-marocaine-de-psa-peugeotcitroen/.*

[19] "Socio-Economic Impact of Ebola Virus Disease in West African Countries: A Call for National and Regional Containment, Recovery and Prevention," New York: United Nations Development Group-Western Central Africa, February 2015, available from *www.africa.undp.org/content/dam/rba/docs/Reports/ebola-westafrica.pdf.*

[20] Rod Mac Johnson, "Ebola Zone Countries Isolated as Airlines Stop Flights," Agence France Presse, October 27, 2014, available from *www.businessinsider.com/afp-ebola-zone-countries-isolatedas-airlines-stop-flights-2014-8.*

[21] "Pays touchés par Ebola: Les chefs d'Etat saluent le soutien du Maroc," ("Countries affected by Ebola: Heads of States Applaud Morocco's support"), *Le Matin*, March 3, 2015, available from *www.lematin.ma/express/2015/pays-touches-par-ebola-_les-chefs- d-etat-saluent-le-soutien-du-maroc/218937.html#sthash.TQuo9ijH. dpuf.*

22 "King Mohammed VI Concludes Four-Country West and Central Africa Tour," Reuters, June 15, 2015, available from *www.reuters.com/article/2015/06/15/idUSnMKWNwLWva+1ec+M KW20150615.*

23 The post-election crisis, which lasted from November 2010 until April 2011, severely disrupted the political, economic, and social fabric of the country. It sparked a displacement of a million of people within the country and also over the border into neighboring countries. The crisis triggered violence and a loss of security, a 3-month shutdown of most banks, the imposition of economic sanctions, heavy weapons combat, and disruption of medications and foodstuffs supplies. For further reading, see Nicolas Cook, "Côte d'Ivoire Post-Gbagbo: Crisis Recovery," Washington, DC: Congressional Research Service, May 3, 2011, available from *fpc.state.gov/documents/organization/164273.pdf.*

24 "Côte d'Ivoire: La filiale d'Attijariwafa bank ferme ses agencies" (Cote d'Ivoire: Atttijarywafa Bank subsidiary closes its Branches"), *Aujourd'hui le Maroc*, April 4, 2011, available from *www.aujourdhui.ma/une/aufildesjours/cote-d-ivoire-la-filiale-d-attijariwafa-bank-ferme-ses-agences-76469#.VZubIMuJiUk.*

25 The crisis started with the December 2012 formation of a coalition of rebel groups known as Seleka that launched an offensive against the government. The crisis escalated in March 2013 with the ousting of President Francois Bozizé and capture of Bangui. For further information, see "The Central African Republic: from Predation to Stabilization," Africa Report No. 219, Washington, DC: International Crisis Group, June 17, 2014, available from *www.crisisgroup.org/~/media/Files/africa/central-africa/central-african-republic/219-la-crise-centrafricaine-de-la-predation-a-la-stabili-sation-english.pdf.*

26 "Annual Report 2013," Angers, France: Banque Populaire, available from *www.gbp.ma/InformationFinanciere/Documents/ InformationsFinancieresDoc/2013/RA-VAng-2013.pdf.*

27 "Report of the Secretary-General on the activities of the United Nations Office for West Africa," S/2015/472, New York: United Nations Security Council, June 24, 2015, available from *www.securitycouncilreport.org/atf/cf/%7B65BFCF9B-6D27-4E9C8CD3-CF6E4FF96FF9%7D/s_2015_472.pdf.*

28 Benjamin Roger, "Maroc : saisie record de 226 kg de cocaïne pure" ("Morocco: record seizure of 226 kg of Pure Cocaine"), *Jeune Afrique*, September 9, 2014, available from *www.jeuneafrique. com/44993/politique/maroc-saisie-record-de-226-kg-de-cocaene-pure/.*

29 "King Mohammed VI's Speech to 69th Session of UN General Assembly," General Debate, available from *www.un.org/en/ ga/69/meetings/gadebate/pdf/MA_en.pdf.*

30 "Hassan Gives Dinner in Honour of Mobuto," *Maghreb Arab Press*, June 21, 1977.

31 Rafael Fraguas, "Sorpresa en Guinea Ecuatorial por la presencia de un contingente militar marroquí," ("Surprise in Equatorial Guinea by the presence of a Moroccan military contingent"), *El Pais*, September 23, 1979, available from *elpais.com/diario/1979/09/23/internacional/306885608_850215.html.*

32 Mountaga Diagne, "Fiche D'Information de L'Etat: Maroc," ("Country Information Sheet: Morocco"), Reseau de Recherche sur leas operations de paix, available from *www.operationspaix. net/115-fiche-d-information-de-l-etat-maroc.html.*

33 Amirah Ibrahim, "Libya: A Critical Review of Tripoli's Sub-Saharan African Policies," Situation Report, Pretoria, South Africa: Institute for Security Studies, November 23, 2009, available from *dspace.africaportal.org/jspui/bitstream/123456789/31021/ 1/23NOV09 LIBYA.pdf?1.* See also Ray Takeyh, "Libya and Africa," Policy Analysis, Washington, DC: The Washington Institute, July 22, 1999, available from *www.washingtoninstitute. org/policy- analysis/view/libya-and-africa.*

[34] E.g., Anne Gearan, "U.S. pushes Algeria to support military intervention in Mali," *The Washington Post*, October 29, 2012, available from *www.washingtonpost.com/world/us-pushes-algeria-tosupport-military-intervention-in-mali/2012/10/29/fee8df44-21a3-11e2-92f8-7f9c4daf276a_story.html.*

[35] Sahel and West Africa Club Secretariat, "Sahel and Maghreb Countries move to strengthen co-operation on security," SWAC News No-142, November 11-17, 2013, available from *www.westafricagateway.org/files/142revuedepresse11-17nov2013_en.pdf.*

[36] The Community of Sahel-Saharan States (CEN-SAD) is an organization that was established in 1999 in Libya, and to which Morocco has been a member since 2001. The General Secretariat is based in Tripoli and its operations have been entirely supported by Libya. The main purpose of CEN-SAD has been to facilitate cooperation among its members, and to achieve economic development, stability and prosperity of member countries. The organization consists of Benin, Burkina Faso, Central African Republic, Chad, the Comoros, Djibouti, Egypt, Eritrea, Gambia, Ghana, Guinea, Guinea Bissau, Ivory Coast, Kenya, Liberia, Libya, Mali, Mauritania, Morocco, Niger, Nigeria, Sao Tome and Principe, Senegal, Somalia, Sierra Leone, Sudan, Togo, and Tunisia. For more information, see "CEN-SAD-The Community of Sahel-Saharan States," New York: United Nations Economic Commission for Africa, available from *www.uneca.org/oria/pages/cen-sad-community-sahel-saharan-states.*

[37] "Communauté des États sahélo-sahariens: Les questions de la sécurité, de la gouvernance et du développement au centre de la réunion de Rabat," ("Community of Sahel-Saharan States: Issues of Security, Governance and Development at the Center of the Rabat Meeting"), *Le Matin*, October 29, 2013, available from *www.lematin.ma/journal/2013/communaute-des-etats-sahelo-sahari-ens_les-questions-de-la-securite-de-la-gouvernance-et-du-developpe-ment-au-centre-de-la-reunion-de-rabat/190260.html#sthash.UF5X-vBxy.dpuf.*

[38] Yahia Zoubir, "Algeria and the Sahelian Imbroglio: Preventing War and Fighting Terrorism," Report, Wadi Al Sail, Qatar: Aljazeera Centre for Studies, November 25, 2012, available from *archives.cerium.ca/IMG/pdf/Algeria_and_the_Sahelian_ Imbroglio_.pdf.*

[39] Jihane Gattioui, "500 imams maliens seront bientôt formés par le Maroc," ("500 Malian imams will soon be formed by Morocco*"), Le Matin*, Febrauary 19, 2014, available from *www.lematin. ma/journal/2014/champ-religieux_500-imams-maliens-seront-bientotformes-par-le-maroc/197137.html#sthash.sWCJmCrI.dpuf.*

[40] "Le Souverain inaugure l'Institut Mohammed VI de formation des imams, morchidines et morchidates dans le cadre des valeurs de l'Islam du juste milieu, pratiqué de tout temps au Maroc," ("The King Inaugurates Mohammed VI Institute for the Training of Imams, Morchidins and Morchidates within the framework of Islamic values of balance that have been always practiced in Morocco"), *Le Matin*, March 27, 2015, available from *www.lematin.ma/journal/2015/le-souverain-inaugure-l-institut-mohammed-vi-de-formation-des-imams-morchidines--et-morchidates-dans-le-cadre-des-valeurs-de-l-islam-du-juste-milieu-pratique-de-tout-temps-au-maroc/220603.html#sthash.nmA1zfSH.dpuf.*

[41] "HM the King, Commander of the Faithful, Chairs Announcement Ceremony of Creation of Mohammed VI Foundation for African Ulemas," Maghreb Arab Press, July 13, 2015, available from *www.mapnews.ma/en/activites-royales/hm-king-com-mander-faithful-chairs-announcement-ceremony-creation-mohammed-vi-found.*

[42] Royal Decree No 1.15.75, Official Gazette N° 6372, June 25, 2015, available from *www.sgg.gov.ma/Portals/0/BO/bulletin/ FR/2015/BO_6374_Fr.pdf.*

[43] Mohammed El-Katiri, "The Institutionalisation of Religious Affairs: Religious Reform in Morocco," *The Journal of North African Studies*, Vol. 18, No. 1, 2013.

44 *Ibid.*

45 "Report of the Secretary-General on the activities of the United Nations Office for West Africa."

46 "US rewards Morocco for terror aid," BBC News, June 4, 2004, available from *news.bbc.co.uk/2/hi/africa/3776413.stm.*

47 "International Military Education and Training: Foreign Military Financing: Peacekeeping Operations," Washington, DC: U.S. Department of State, undated document, available from *www.state.gov/documents/organization/60649.pdf.*

48 "NATO: Morocco, a Strategic Partner, Mediterranean Dialogue Driving Force," Morocco World News, March 12, 2015, available from *www.moroccoworldnews.com/2015/03/153787/natomorocco-strategic-partner-mediterranean-dialogue-driving-force/.*

49 "SNMG2 trains with Royal Moroccan Navy," Northwood, Middlesex, UK: NATO Allied Maritime Command, April 7, 2015, available from *www.aco.nato.int/snmg2-trains-with-royal-moroccannavy.aspx.*

ABOUT THE AUTHOR

MOHAMMED EL-KATIRI is a Director of MENA Insight, a political risk consultancy that focuses on the Middle East and North Africa, and a Senior Research Analyst at the United Kingdom's (UK) Conflict Studies Research Centre (CSRC). Before joining CSRC, Dr. El-Katiri was a Research Fellow at the UK Defence Academy, and later served as a Political Risk Analyst at Eurasia Group and as a senior researcher at the Hague Institute for Global Justice. With more than 10 years of regional experience, his research interests include political and economic security in North Africa and the Gulf Cooperation Council (GCC) states, as well as North African relations with the European Union (EU), and security policies around the Mediterranean. Dr. El-Katiri has published numerous internal and external UK Defence Academy reports, including reference papers on national and regional security issues in the GCC and the Mediterranean, and a monograph on the Algerian national oil and gas company Sonatrach. In addition, his publications include commentaries and research papers in a range of languages for research organizations in the UK and Europe, as well as various newspaper articles in and about the region. Dr. El-Katiri is a frequent commentator in media including the British Broadcasting Company (BBC), the *Financial Times*, and *Al-Jazeera*.

In: Morocco
Editor: Wilson Graves

ISBN: 978-1-63485-107-7

Chapter 3

MOROCCO 2014 HUMAN RIGHTS REPORT*

U.S. Department of State; Bureau of Democracy, Human Rights and Labor

EXECUTIVE SUMMARY

Morocco is a monarchy with a constitution under which ultimate authority rests with King Mohammed VI, who presides over the Council of Ministers. The king may dismiss ministers, dissolve parliament, and call for new elections or rule by decree. International and domestic observers judged the 2011 parliamentary elections credible and relatively free from irregularities. The Islamist Party of Justice and Development (PJD) won a plurality of seats in the 2011 elections. As mandated by the constitution, the king chose the PJD to lead the governing coalition. Authorities failed at times to maintain effective control over security forces.

The most significant continuing human rights problems were the lack of citizens' ability to change the constitutional provisions establishing the country's monarchical form of government, corruption in all branches of government, and widespread disregard for the rule of law by security forces.

---

* This is an edited, reformatted and augmented version of a report issued by the U.S. Department of State; Bureau of Democracy, Human Rights and Labor, June 2015.

A variety of sources reported other human rights problems. These included security forces committing human rights abuses on multiple occasions. The UN Human Rights Council's Working Group on Arbitrary Detention detected "a systematic pattern of acts of torture and ill-treatment during the arrest and detention process." Prison and detention conditions were substandard. The judiciary lacked independence, and pretrial detention frequently exceeded what the law allows. Domestic and international nongovernmental organizations (NGOs) asserted there were political prisoners, many of whom were detained under the antiterrorism law. Police used excessive force to quell peaceful protests, resulting in hundreds of injuries. The government abridged civil liberties by infringing on freedom of speech and press, limiting freedom of assembly and association, and restricting the right to practice one's religion. There was discrimination against women and girls. Trafficking in persons and child labor continued to occur, particularly in the informal sector.

There were few examples and no high-profile reports of investigations or prosecutions of abuse or corruption, whether in the security services or elsewhere in the government, contributing to the widespread perception of impunity.

SECTION 1. RESPECT FOR THE INTEGRITY OF THE PERSON, INCLUDING FREEDOM FROM

a. Arbitrary or Unlawful Deprivation of Life

There were no reports that the government or its agents committed arbitrary or unlawful killings.

b. Disappearance

There were no reported cases of politically motivated disappearance during the year. An August 4 report from the UN Working Group on Arbitrary Detention stated it had received accusations "from sources deemed to be credible" that disappearances continued to occur in direct violation of Article 23 of the constitution, which provides for humane treatment of prisoners and detainees, although it did not give specific examples.

Regarding unresolved cases of disappearance dating to the 1970s and 1980s, the National Council on Human Rights (CNDH), created and funded by the government, continued to investigate claims of enforced and involuntary disappearance and, when warranted, recommended reparations in the form of money, health care, employment, or vocational training. In 2012 the government paid 43 million dirhams ($5.2 million) to 345 beneficiaries. The CNDH continued to shift its activities to community reparation projects and supported 107 projects focused on women's empowerment, income generation, and preservation of the environment in 13 provinces, but not in Western Sahara. The CNDH continued to review open claims for reparation and occasionally received new claims, especially in Western Sahara. (See the Western Sahara report for more information on reparation claims in the territory.)

Human rights groups representing Sahrawis, an ethnic minority living throughout the country and constituting the majority of the population of Western Sahara at the time of the disappearances, voiced concern over the slow pace at which the CNDH addressed outstanding and new claims. An association of victims and their families, the Sahrawi Association of Victims of Grave Human Rights Abuses (ASVDH), claimed at least 114 cases remained unresolved at the end of 2012 and accused the government and the CNDH of failing to acknowledge additional cases of disappearance that occurred between 1956 and 1999, especially from Western Sahara.

c. Torture and Other Cruel, Inhuman, or Degrading Treatment or Punishment

The constitution and the law prohibit such practices, and the government denied it used torture. Numerous credible accounts of cruel, inhuman, or degrading treatment of prisoners and detainees, however, confirmed the existence of "a pattern of torture and mistreatment," particularly in cases related to state security. In his April 2013 report to the UN Human Rights Council, Special Rapporteur Juan Mendez welcomed the "development of an emerging culture of human rights in Morocco," but noted that torture and mistreatment still occurred. An August 4 report by the UN Working Group on Detention found that the use of torture was systematic in certain cases involving terrorism and state security.

In December 2013, at the invitation of the government, the UN Working Group on Arbitrary Detention visited prisons in Sale, Tangier, Tetouan,

Casablanca, and Laayoune in Western Sahara. The group's August 4 report stated that "in cases related to State security, such as cases involving terrorism, membership in Islamist movements or supporters of independence for Western Sahara, the Working Group on Arbitrary Detention found that there was a pattern of torture and mistreatment during arrest and in detention by police officers, in particular agents of the National Surveillance Directorate." In 2012, after an eight-day visit, UN Special Rapporteur on Torture Juan E. Mendez stated that he had received credible testimonies of "undue physical and mental pressure of detainees in the course of interrogations." He noted in his report on the visit that "acts of torture and ill-treatment during the detention and arrest process" were "frequently linked to large demonstrations, a perceived threat to national security, or terrorism."

In a 2012 report, the CNDH noted that it had observed a "persistence of abuses by the staff of visited prisons against inmates." The CNDH further indicated that prison staff beat prisoners with sticks and hoses, hung them on doors with handcuffs, beat the soles of their feet, slapped them, pricked them with needles, burned them, kicked them, forced them to undress in view of other prisoners, and used insults and malicious language against them. The CNDH noted that abuses persisted in most of the prisons it visited, except for Inezgane and Dakhla, "where only isolated cases were witnessed." Numerous NGO reports and media articles reinforced these points with accounts of security force members torturing and abusing individuals in their custody, particularly during pretrial detention.

The law against torture requires judges to refer a detainee to a forensic medical expert when the detainee or his or her lawyer requests it, or if judges notice suspicious physical marks on a detainee. The UN Working Group on Arbitrary Detention, human rights NGOs, and the media documented prominent cases of authorities' failure to implement provisions of the antitorture law.

In his April 2013 report, the special rapporteur noted the "apparent absence" of investigations, prosecutions, and remedies "in all cases of torture and ill-treatment." According to government-provided data, there were four cases presented to the legal system during the year of alleged police torture, although specific examples were not given.

In two cases, defendants received two- and three-year sentences and a fine for "false allegations of torture" and "reporting a crime that the complainant knows has not been committed." On July 23, a court sentenced Oussama Housne, a member of the Moroccan Association of Human Rights (AMDH), to three years' imprisonment and to pay compensation to the police of 100,000 dirhams ($12,000) for a false torture report and slander. On October 20, an appellate court in Tangier increased the sentence of Wafae Charaf, a human rights and political activist, to two years in prison and a 1,000 dirham fine ($120) for allegedly falsely reporting being abducted and tortured by unknown persons on April 27. The court ordered her to pay 50,000 dirhams ($6,000) in compensation to the police force for slander.

There was progress in eradicating the practice of torture. In two instances there were reports of investigations begun by authorities. In August the appellate court in Agadir dismissed a lower court conviction on the grounds that medical examiners found the defendant to have been subjected to torture; the officer in charge of the interrogation was reportedly under investigation. On November 10, Minister of Justice Mustafa Ramid directed the General Inspection of his ministry to open an investigation against a local prosecutor in Kenitra after it was revealed that he had denied a medical review to students who had claimed to have been tortured while detained earlier that month. No further information on the status of either investigation was available at year's end.

During the year there were numerous incidents of security forces' use of excessive force against largely peaceful demonstrations organized by the February 20 Movement and by groups of unemployed university graduates (see section 2.b.). On April 6, security forces in Casablanca used violence against a large protest composed of unionists, unemployed university graduates, and February 20 Movement members. Security forces arrested 11 protesters, whom authorities later charged with violence against law enforcement agents and participating in an unauthorized protest.

Some international organizations, such as Amnesty International (AI), continued to claim that torture occurred at police administrative facilities, where police maintained detention cells.

PRISON AND DETENTION CENTER CONDITIONS

Prison conditions remained poor and generally did not meet international standards.

Physical Conditions: The government stated that its 76 prisons held 62,775 inmates as of June. Prisons were overcrowded, resulting in poor hygiene and inadequate nutrition for prisoners. Due to overcrowding, authorities frequently held pretrial detainees and convicted prisoners together, with an average of 18 square feet of cell space per prisoner. There was no information available concerning the availability of potable water. According to the CNDH, prison facilities did not provide adequate access to health care and did not accommodate the needs of prisoners with disabilities, although government sources claimed each prisoner received an average of 3.4 consultations with a medical professional during the first seven months of the year. The Moroccan Observatory of Prisons (OMP), an umbrella group of lawyers promoting better prison conditions, along with human rights NGOs and a parliamentary commission, continued to report that prisons were overcrowded, prone to violence, and failed to meet local and international standards.

The government reported that 93 inmates, 83 of whom were hospitalized, died in prison during the year. Local human rights NGOs were unable to confirm these numbers. The government acknowledged that providing adequate care was difficult in overcrowded conditions. During the year a local magazine, *Telquel*, released an investigative report on prisons, noting that about half of all detainees were incarcerated in a state of "preventive detention," with that number reaching 87 percent of the inmates in some prisons, such as Oukacha in Casablanca.

The law provides for the separation of minors, but a significant number of children, some as young as 14, were held with adults, particularly in pretrial detention in ordinary prisons and in police stations, due to the lack of juvenile prison facilities. The government reserved three detention facilities, known officially as reform and education centers, exclusively for juveniles up to the age of 20. Several other adult prison facilities had dedicated areas for juvenile inmates. NGOs provided education and rehabilitation services for juvenile inmates, while the government provided the majority of vocational and educational training through various agencies, such as the Ministry of Education. NGOs also provided some recreational activities. According to the government, 4,331 juveniles under the age of 20 were imprisoned as of August. Human rights groups reported that other minors, older inmates, and prison guards abused young offenders, including sexually. Government figures indicated that fewer than 3 percent of prisoners were women; there was less overcrowding in the women's sections of gender-segregated facilities.

Administration: The Directorate General for Prison Administration, a separate agency that reports directly to the prime minister and informally to the king, has responsibility for managing all prisons and detention centers in the country. It has its own budget and central administrative apparatus.

The Ministry of Justice directs the development and reform of penal policy. Prison administration recordkeeping was adequate, but there were serious irregularities in the records, particularly in the administrative records of those in police custody. The CNDH acted as an ombudsman for human rights. The CNDH received complaints from prisoners and from individuals writing on behalf of imprisoned family members (see section 1.e.). In several instances the CNDH intervened directly with authorities to seek royal pardons or address poor detention conditions.

Authorities did not implement alternatives to imprisonment for nonviolent offenders.

While authorities permitted relatives and friends to visit prisoners, there were reports they denied this privilege in some instances. Family members of prisoners accounted for the vast majority of prison visits, which were occasionally made more difficult by the transfer of prisoners to distant prisons for disciplinary reasons.

Government policy permits NGOs that provide social, educational, or religious services to prisoners to enter prison facilities, but it does not permit entry to NGOs with only a human rights mandate, except with special authorization. Prisoners and detainees could practice their religions. The OMP and members of government-recognized NGOs, including the Moroccan Organization for Human Rights, visited prisoners regularly to distribute food and personal items and to check on their well-being as "friends or family" rather than as representatives of human rights NGOs. According to prison authorities, 356 visits by domestic NGOs and 65 visits by the CNDH occurred during the year.

In February a system of "letterboxes" was introduced in prisons to facilitate prisoners' right to submit complaints regarding their imprisonment. The government reported it registered 1,879 complaints from prisoners between January and August. There was no information available on whether prisoners could submit complaints to judicial authorities without censorship or whether authorities investigated and made public credible allegations of inhuman conditions and treatment. From January to August, the prison authority disciplined its staff in 62 instances, with penalties ranging from a warning to dismissal.

Some human rights activists asserted the prison administration reserved harsher treatment for Islamists. A 2012 CNDH report confirmed the "abusive use of administrative transfer as a disciplinary measure" for Salafi jihadist detainees. The government denied allegations that it accorded different levels of treatment to any inmates.

Prisoners frequently employed hunger strikes to demand improved prison conditions or protest lengthy pretrial detentions. Most of these hunger strikes ended within several days due to concessions from the government or prison authorities. Although prison authorities provided meals to prisoners three times per day, the amount of food was insufficient. Prisoners regularly relied on families and friends for sufficient nutrition.

The government continued vocational and educational training programs in prisons. The Mohammed VI Foundation for the Reinsertion of Prisoners provided educational and professional training to young inmates on the verge of release. The foundation continued to run reform and education centers in 50 of the country's 76 prisons and worked with 17,991 prisoners. In addition, the foundation provided programs for former prisoners' "personal reinsertion" at its Centers for Post-Incarceration Support.

Independent Monitoring: The government did not permit independent nongovernmental human rights observers or local human rights groups to make unaccompanied prison-monitoring visits.

d. Arbitrary Arrest or Detention

The constitution prohibits arbitrary arrest and detention. Nonetheless, the UN Human Rights Council's Working Group on Arbitrary Detention and other observers indicated that police did not respect these provisions or consistently observe due process. According to local NGOs and associations, police sometimes arrested persons without warrants, held detainees beyond the statutory deadline to charge them, and failed to identify themselves when making arrests.

Role of the Police and Security Apparatus

The security apparatus includes several police and paramilitary organizations with overlapping authority. The National Police manage internal law enforcement and report to the Ministry of Interior. The Auxiliary Forces also report to the Ministry of Interior and support gendarmes and police. The Royal Gendarmerie, which reports to the Administration of National Defense, is responsible for law enforcement in rural regions and on national highways. Both the Royal Gendarmerie and the judicial police report to the royal prosecutor. The Department of Royal Security is a branch of the National Police and reports to the king.

Civilian authorities failed at times to maintain effective control over the security forces, and there were credible reports of abuses and impunity. Systemic higher-level corruption, as well as pervasive corruption, undermined law enforcement and the effectiveness of the judicial system. Authorities provided no official data about government investigation, prosecution, or punishment of officials who committed such abuses.

Impunity was pervasive in the absence of effective mechanisms to investigate and punish abuse and corruption. Authorities investigated very few incidents of alleged abuse and corruption, and there was no systematic prosecution of security personnel who committed human rights abuses. Cases often languished in the investigatory or trial phases. In one investigation into corruption among Casablanca police early in the year, 24 officers were presented with a choice of resigning or facing justice, and the majority chose to resign.

ARREST PROCEDURES AND TREATMENT OF DETAINEES

Police may arrest an individual after a general prosecutor issues an oral or written warrant. The law provides for access to a lawyer in the first 24 hours after arrest in ordinary criminal cases, but that provision was not consistently respected. The law permits authorities to deny defendants' access to counsel or family members during the initial 96 hours of detention under terrorism-related laws or during the initial 24 hours of detention for other charges, with an optional extension of 12 hours with the approval of the Prosecutor's Office. Abuse or torture generally occurred during these initial detention periods, when police interrogated detainees.

Under terrorism-related laws, a prosecutor may renew the initial detention period twice by written authorization, for a total detention time of 12 days. According to the Antiterrorism Act, there is no right to a lawyer during this time except for a half-hour monitored visit at the midpoint of the 12-day period (see section 1.d.).

NGO sources stated that some judges were reticent to use alternative sentences permitted under the law, such as provisional release. The law does not require written authorization for release from detention. In some instances judges released defendants on their own recognizance. According to the law, all defendants have the right to attorneys; if a defendant cannot afford private counsel, a court-appointed attorney must be provided when the criminal penalty exceeds five years in prison. Authorities did not always provide effective counsel. In nonterrorism cases, the law requires police to notify a detainee's next of kin of the arrest as soon as possible after the initial 36-hour period of incommunicado detention, unless arresting authorities applied for and received an extension from a magistrate. Police did not consistently abide by this provision. Because authorities sometimes delayed notifying the family, lawyers were not informed promptly of the date of arrest and were not able to monitor compliance with detention limits and treatment of the detainee. Under a separate military code, military authorities may detain members of the military without a warrant or public trial.

Arbitrary Arrest: Security forces often arrested groups of individuals, took them to a police station, questioned them for several hours, and released them without charge.

The August 4 report of the UN Working Group on Arbitrary Detention noted that undocumented migrants have been arrested, detained, and escorted to the borders or otherwise expelled without an opportunity to exercise their rights, contrary to law. The government failed to provide persons awaiting deportation--who were not under the authority of the prison system--with information about the reasons for their arrest or conditions of their detention (see section 2.d.).

Pretrial Detention: Although the government claimed that accused persons were generally brought to trial within two months, prosecutors may request as many as five additional two-month extensions of pretrial detention. Pretrial detentions could last as long as one year, and there were reports that authorities routinely held detainees beyond the one-year limit. Government officials attributed these delays to the large backlog of cases in the justice system. The Foreign Ministry stated that a variety of factors contributed to this backlog: a lack of resources devoted to the justice system, both human and infrastructure; the lack of plea bargaining as an option for prosecutors, lengthening the amount of time to process cases on average; and the scant use of mediation and other out-of-court settlement mechanisms allowed by law. In a report published during the year, the International Federation of Human Rights estimated that approximately 50 percent of detainees were in pretrial detention. In some cases detainees received a sentence shorter than the time they spent in pretrial detention. NGOs continued to report that more than half of incarcerated minors were in pretrial detention. In some cases authorities detained minors for as long as eight months prior to trial.

Amnesty: The king continued selectively to exercise his ability to grant pardons to those convicted of crimes. The decision-making process for granting royal pardons remained opaque. By August 21, according to government figures, the king had granted 12,171 releases from prison; the number of pardons in total was unknown.

e. Denial of Fair Public Trial

The constitution provides for an independent judiciary, but the courts were not independent. Government officials, NGOs, and lawyers widely acknowledged that corruption and extrajudicial influence weakened judicial independence.

Authorities sometimes failed to respect court orders. For example, the 2005 court order to register ASVDH remained unenforced at year's end. Nonetheless, in some cases the judiciary demonstrated impartiality. In a November lawsuit against the Ministry of Interior, the court awarded AMDH 100,000 dirhams ($12,000) in damages for the "baseless" prohibition of a demonstration organized by the association in September.

TRIAL PROCEDURES

Defendants are presumed innocent. The law provides for the right to a fair public trial with the right of appeal, but this did not always occur, especially for those protesting the incorporation of Western Sahara into the country. Juries are not used. Attorneys, particularly in juvenile matters, indicated that, while clients frequently maintained their innocence, judges passed over the question of culpability and focused on sentencing.

Defendants have the right to be present at their trial and to timely consultation with an attorney. In practice lawyers were often denied timely access to their clients and, in the majority of cases, met them only at the first hearing before the judge.

Attorneys were not appointed in all cases or, if provided at public expense, were poorly paid. Defense attorneys were often not properly trained in matters pertaining to juveniles or not provided in a timely fashion, often resulting in inadequate representation. Many NGOs provided attorneys for minors, who frequently did not have the means to pay. Such resources were limited and specific to larger cities. By law defendants in criminal and human rights cases have access to government evidence against them, but judges sometimes prevented or delayed access. The law permits defense attorneys to question witnesses. Despite the provisions of the law, some judges reportedly denied defense requests to question witnesses or to present mitigating witnesses or evidence.

The law forbids judges from admitting confessions made under duress. In its August 4 report, the UN Working Group on Arbitrary Detention noted that "many" individuals in detention were convicted and sentenced to prison solely based on confessions obtained under duress. Human Rights Watch (HRW) and local NGOs charged that judges, at their discretion, decided cases based on forced confessions. NGOs alleged this occurred frequently in cases against Sahrawis or individuals accused of terrorism. According to authorities, police claims about detainees' statements were sometimes used in place of defendants' confessions when there was a possible question of duress. In its June 2013 report on unfair trials based on confession, HRW concluded that judges and prosecutors continually rejected or refused to open inquiries into complaints of police abuse and mistreatment. The serious lack of medical, forensic, and psychiatric expertise made it practically impossible to gather credible evidence of mistreatment that would be admissible in court.

POLITICAL PRISONERS AND DETAINEES

The law does not define or recognize the concept of a political prisoner. The government did not consider any of its prisoners to be political prisoners and stated that all individuals in prison had been convicted or had been charged under criminal law. Criminal law, however, covers nonviolent advocacy and dissent, such as insulting police in songs or "defaming Morocco's sacred values" by denouncing the king and regime during a public demonstration. In addition, NGOs, including the Moroccan Association for Human Rights, Sahrawi organizations, and Amazigh activist groups, asserted that the government imprisoned persons for political activities or beliefs under the cover of criminal charges. For example, on April 6, police arrested 11 members of the February 20 Movement in Casablanca for "organizing an unauthorized union" with the three largest unions in the country. They were sentenced on May 22, with some members receiving prison sentences and others receiving heavy fines. According to NGOs, approximately 40 political prisoners, many of them members of the February 20 Movement, remained in prison at year's end.

Civil Judicial Procedures and Remedies

Although individuals have access to civil courts for lawsuits relating to human rights violations and have filed lawsuits, such lawsuits were frequently unsuccessful due to the courts' lack of independence or impartiality stemming from extrajudicial influence and corruption. There are administrative as well as judicial remedies for alleged wrongs.

A National Ombudsman's Office (Mediator Institution) helped to resolve civil matters when the judiciary was unable to do so and has gradually expanded the scope of its activities. In 2013 the office received 9,431 complaints, of which 1,920 fell within the mediator's purview and were subject to in-depth investigation. Authorities retransmitted to the CNDH for resolution 43 cases specifically related to allegations of human rights abuses against authorities. The CNDH continued to be a conduit through which citizens expressed complaints about human rights abuses and violations.

f. Arbitrary Interference with Privacy, Family, Home, or Correspondence

While the constitution states an individual's home is inviolable and that a search may take place only with a search warrant, authorities at times entered homes without judicial authorization, monitored without legal process personal movement and private communications--including e-mail, text messaging, or other digital communications intended to remain private--and employed informers.

Section 2. Respect for Civil Liberties, Including

a. Freedom of Speech and Press

The law generally provides for freedom of speech and press, although it criminalizes and restricts some freedom of expression, particularly in the press and social media. Government-provided figures for 2012 showed that 45 journalists or media outlets faced criminal or civil charges, a decrease from previous years. This number included cases that the government initiated as well as private citizens' libel complaints. Numerous human rights groups criticized the steady stream of criminal prosecutions of journalists and publishers as well as of libel suits.

Freedom of Speech: The law criminalizes and the government actively prosecutes persons who criticize Islam, the institution of the monarchy, state institutions, officials such as those in the military, and the government's official position regarding territorial integrity and claim to Western Sahara.

There were multiple incidents of outspoken February 20 Movement supporters and activists being arrested under dubious criminal charges rather than under libel or other free speech-related charges. In March 2013 authorities released rapper Mouad Belghouat after serving a one-year prison sentence for insulting a public official in the video accompanying his song, "Dogs of the State." On May 18, police rearrested him at a soccer match in Casablanca and accused him of scalping tickets. Although authorities later dropped the charges, a court convicted him of public intoxication and insulting a police officer and sentenced him to four months in prison and a fine of 15,500 dirhams ($1,880). Belghouat's defense withdrew from the court before sentencing to protest the court's refusal to allow defense witnesses.

Press Freedoms: The antiterrorism law and press code include provisions that permit the government to jail and impose financial penalties on journalists and publishers who violate restrictions related to defamation, libel, and insults. Prison sentences may be imposed on those convicted of libel. The press, consequently, reported gingerly on controversial and culturally sensitive topics involving the military and national security. Self-censorship and government restrictions on sensitive topics remained serious hurdles to the development of a free, independent, and investigative press. Authorities filed charges of libel and other violations of the criminal code against specific journalists, with prosecution of these charges indefinitely delayed. For example, on June 13, a court sentenced Toufik Bouachrine, editor of the daily newspaper *Akhbar Al Youm*, to a six-month suspended sentence and a fine of 10,000 dirhams ($1,200) for swindling in connection with a 2007 real estate case. Although a trial court and an appellate court had found Bouachrine innocent on the swindling charge, the case was reopened at the same time that charges were brought regarding a caricature of a member of the royal family that he had published in his newspaper. In an editorial for the newspaper, Bouachrine reaffirmed his belief that the retrial was politically motivated.

In September 2013 authorities charged journalist Ali Anouzla under the antiterrorism law with "inciting terrorism" for linking to a video hosted by third parties and produced by al Qaida in the Islamic Maghreb. In October 2013 authorities granted Anouzla a "provisional" release from prison. On May 29, an appeals court sentenced him to a month in prison and a fine of 5,000 dirhams ($600).

Violence and Harassment: Authorities subjected some journalists to harassment and intimidation, including attempts to discredit them through rumors about their personal life. Journalists reported that selective prosecutions served as a mechanism for intimidation.

Censorship or Content Restrictions: While the government rarely censored the domestic press, it exerted pressure by pursing legal cases that resulted in serious financial problems for proprietors due to heavy fines and suspensions of publication. The consequences in prior years destroyed the financial viability of some publications; memory of those examples encouraged editors and journalists to self-censor. The press code lists threats to public order as one of the criteria for censorship. Publications and broadcast media must also obtain government accreditation. The government has the ability to deny and revoke accreditation as well as to suspend or confiscate publications.

Libel Laws/National Security: The antiterrorism law provides for the arrest of journalists and the filtering of websites deemed to "disrupt public order by intimidation, terror, or violence." In July 2013 a court sentenced journalist and human rights activist Mostafa al-Hesnawi to four years' imprisonment for "creating a terrorist organization that threatens national security and stability." In October 2013 a Rabat appeals court subsequently reduced his sentence to three years. Hesnawi previously criticized authorities' use of antiterrorism laws against individuals not involved in terrorist activities. In May, Hesnawi began a hunger strike to raise the profile of his case; 72 days later, on August 14, he died while incarcerated in Fes from complications of his hunger strike.

Internet Freedom

The government applied laws and restrictions governing speech and the press to the internet in a nontransparent manner. There are neither specific laws nor a body of judicial decisions concerning internet content or access. Individuals and groups self-censored and generally were careful to adhere to restrictions on expression and, accordingly, to engage in peaceful exchanges of views via the internet, including by e-mail. The government monitored private online communications on the internet and collected personally identifiable information in connection with citizens' peaceful expression of political, religious, or ideological opinion or beliefs.

In 2013, according to the World Bank, approximately 2.5 percent of households subscribed to fixed broadband services and 56 percent of the population used the internet.

ACADEMIC FREEDOM AND CULTURAL EVENTS

By law the government has the right to criminalize presentations or debate questioning the legitimacy of the monarchy, Islam, state institutions, or the status of Western Sahara. The law restricts cultural events and academic activities, although the government generally provided more latitude to political and religious activism confined to university campuses. The Ministry of Interior approved appointments of university rectors in keeping with the Organic Law on Nominations to High Functions.

b. Freedom of Peaceful Assembly and Association

The constitution provides for the freedoms of assembly and association subject to restrictions provided by law.

FREEDOM OF ASSEMBLY

The law conditions the right to assemble publicly on acquiring Ministry of Interior permission. Some NGOs complained that authorities did not apply the approval process consistently. The government used administrative delays and other methods to suppress or discourage unwanted peaceful assembly as well as excessive force to disperse demonstrations. Groups of more than three persons require authorization to assemble. In the absence of this authorization, authorities disbanded meetings organized by groups ranging from reformers to the national union of judges, sometimes with excessive force.

According to HRW, authorities blocked more than 15 meetings that the Moroccan Human Rights Association tried to hold in the country since July. Authorities also denied venues for events planned by the Moroccan League for Human Rights, AI, and other civil society organizations. Authorities reportedly searched the homes of members of the Justice and Charity Organization, a Sufi charitable group the government tolerated but did not officially recognize, who were allowing their houses to be used for politically oriented meetings. Group members claimed that the Ministry of Interior's General Directorate of Territorial Surveillance harassed attendees. While several homes remained sealed, there were no new reports of homes being sealed during the year. In almost every case, authorities released Justice and Charity Organization members without charges after detention and questioning.

Authorities restricted AI's activities in the country, actions which observers believed were tied to AI's launch of its global campaign for the abolition of torture in May. In September authorities prohibited AI from hosting an annual youth camp in Bouznika; in October, they refused entry to an AI delegation seeking to gather information on immigrants and refugees.

Protests occurred on a nearly weekly basis throughout the year. In one example, on November 3 the Arabic-language daily *Akhbar Al Youm Al Maghrebiya* reported that dozens of activists from the AMDH were to take to the streets to protest the actions of the Ministry of Interior in banning 17 of their activities. Authorities tolerated most demonstrations by unemployed university graduates and unions, even if they were unauthorized. NGOs reported that both plainclothes and uniformed state security agents monitored human rights events.

Violence erupted between security forces and protesters in instances documented in the media. For example, on April 6, security forces in Casablanca used violence to disperse a large protest that was mainly initiated and led by members of the February 20 Movement. The protest resulted in the arrest of 11 protesters who were later charged with violence against law enforcement officers. In another example, on November 27, students from the Islamist movement Justice and Charity attempted to conduct a sit-in in front of the parliament building. Police rapidly dispersed the students and detained 12. No explanation was given, although security forces previously stated they would intervene in the case of unauthorized demonstrations.

Freedom of Association

The constitution and the law provide for freedom of association, although the government placed severe restrictions on this freedom. The government prohibited or failed to recognize political opposition groups by deeming them unqualified for NGO status. According to HRW's *World Report 2014*, citizens continued to hold marches and rallies to demand political reform and protest government actions since popular protests swept the region in 2011. Police allowed most of these protests, but on some occasions they attacked and severely beat protesters.

The Ministry of the Interior required NGOs to register, but there was no comprehensive national register publicly available. A prospective organization must submit its objectives, bylaws, address, and photocopies of members' identification cards to the ministry. The ministry issues a receipt to the organization that signifies formal approval. If the organization does not receive a receipt within 60 days, it is not formally registered. The government denied official recognition to NGOs that it considered as advocating against the monarchy, Islam as the state religion, or territorial integrity. Several organizations the government chose not to recognize functioned without the receipts, and the government tolerated their activities, including the ASVDH. The ASVDH won an administrative court judgment confirming that its applications for registration conformed to the law, although administrative courts have no enforcement powers.

Authorities did not permit registration of organizations supporting self-determination for Western Sahara, including the ASVDH. Unregistered organizations could not access government funds or legally accept contributions.

Authorities continued to monitor Justice and Charity Organization activities.

c. Freedom of Religion

See the Department of State's *International Religious Freedom Report* at www.state.gov/j/drl/irf/rpt/.

d. Freedom of Movement, Internally Displaced Persons, Protection of Refugees, and Stateless Persons

In-country Movement: The law provides for freedom of internal movement. Authorities generally respected this right, although the government restricted movement in areas regarded as militarily sensitive, including the demilitarized zone in Western Sahara.

Exile: While the law provides for forced exile, there were no instances of forced exile during the year.

Emigration and Repatriation: The government encouraged the return of Sahrawi refugees if they acknowledged the government's authority over Western Sahara. The government continued to make travel documents available to Sahrawis, and there were no reported cases of Sahrawis being prevented from traveling (see the Western Sahara report).

PROTECTION OF REFUGEES

The government cooperated with the Office of the UN High Commissioner for Refugees (UNHCR) and other humanitarian organizations in providing protection and assistance to internally displaced persons, refugees, returning refugees, asylum seekers, stateless persons, and other persons of concern. The UNHCR registered 854 refugees and asylum seekers during the year. Of these, 266 were Syrian citizens. On November 14, members of a government committee designed to reconstitute the government's Office for Refugees and Stateless Persons stated that they had processed and interviewed 517 of the UNHCR-recognized refugees, a figure that the UNHCR subsequently confirmed; the government had not yet located the remaining individuals. The committee approved 509 of the 517 individuals for refugee status. Government officials determined that the remaining eight interviewees from the group--mostly children with a Moroccan parent--were entitled to Moroccan citizenship and therefore ineligible for refugee status in Morocco. On December 18, the Council of Government announced its decision to adopt the *National Strategy on Migration and Asylum* elaborated by the Ministry in Charge of Moroccans Living Abroad and Migration Affairs "to better respond to the challenges of managing migration issues."

Access to Asylum: The law provides for refugee status. The government has historically deferred to the UNHCR as the sole agency in the country entitled to grant refugee status and verify asylum cases. The commission charged with the regularization of UNHCR-recognized refugees completed the cases of 545 refugees during the year. The government recognized two types of asylum status: refugees designated according to the UNHCR statute and the "exceptional regularization of persons in irregular situation." The latter was part of an overall government effort to provide some status to its large transitory migrant population. To that effect, from the beginning of the year through September 9, the government granted status to more than 5,000 of the 17,757 individuals who had applied and issued more than 3,000 residence cards.

Refugee Abuse: Refugees and asylum seekers, as well as migrants, were particularly vulnerable to abuse. There were periodic reports, particularly in the north, of mass arrests and brutalization by security forces of sub-Saharan migrants and of abuse by criminal gangs involved in human trafficking. There were credible reports of government authorities arresting, detaining, and expelling irregular migrants, particularly at the border town of Oujda and also into the desert along the border with Algeria, where some were abandoned without food and water (see section 1.d.).

The UNHCR reported arrests of migrants and asylum seekers during the year, and NGOs reported that migrants were at times deported without recourse to legal counsel and sometimes to countries other than their country of their origin. The migrant rights organization Antiracism Group for the Protection of Foreigners and Migrants reported an increase in the number of arrests of illegal migrants during the year as well as an increase in violence and aggression by both the government and migrant populations. In September the August 30 killing on the outskirts of Tangier of a Senegalese migrant with legal status in Morocco sparked protests and drew international attention to the violence and discrimination that sub-Saharan African immigrants faced.

Access to Basic Services: Recognized refugees were able to gain access to health care services. Asylum seekers were, however, often unable to access the national health-care system and continued to have little access to the judicial system. During the year the Ministry of National Education and Professional Training released a circular stating its intention to provide the children of refugees, migrants, and asylum seekers with access to the education system, which was partially implemented in larger cities by year's end.

Section 3. Respect for Political Rights: The Right of Citizens to Change Their Government

Citizens do not have the ability to change the constitutional provisions establishing the country's monarchical form of government. The law provides for, and citizens participated in, regular, free elections based on universal suffrage for parliament's Chamber of Representatives and municipal councils.

Parliament's Chamber of Counselors and the regional councils are indirectly elected.

The king may dissolve parliament in consultation with the head of government (prime minister) and can rule by decree. As head of state, the king appoints the head of government. The king presides over the Council of Ministers, the supreme decision-making body, except in cases when he delegates that authority to the head of government. Constitutional changes outlining this division of responsibility came into effect in 2011. On July 31, an organic law institutionalized the right of parliament to establish ad hoc fact-finding committees, but none was established by year's end. Nevertheless, the decision-making authority of the prime minister and parliament remained unclear.

Matters of security, strategic policy, and religion remain within the purview of the king, who presides over the Supreme Security Council and the Ulema Council (Council of Senior Religious Scholars). The constitution obliges the king to choose the prime minister from the party with the most elected seats in the Chamber of Representatives. The constitution authorizes the prime minister to nominate all government ministers, although they serve at the king's pleasure since he has the power to dismiss them. Royal advisors worked closely in undefined coordinating roles with government ministries.

The constitution can be amended when proposals are approved by national referendum and approved by the king, or when the king submits a bill that receives two-thirds majority approval from both legislative chambers.

Elections and Political Participation

Recent Elections: In the 2011 parliamentary elections, which saw a turnout of approximately 45 percent, the Islamist PJD won 107 of the 395 seats in 92 constituencies. Of the 395 seats, 60 were reserved for women and 30 for individuals under the age of 40.

The major political parties and the vast majority of the 3,500 domestic observers considered the elections free, fair, and transparent. Most international observers considered them to be credible elections in which voters were able to choose freely and deemed the process relatively free of irregularities.

Political Parties: Political parties faced fewer government-imposed restrictions under the revised constitution. The Ministry of Interior applied new laws that made it easier for political parties to register. A political party may not legally challenge the institution of the monarchy, Islam as the state religion, or the country's territorial integrity. No party may be legally based in a religious, ethnic, or regional identity.

Participation of Women and Minorities: Female politicians featured prominently in the press on a variety of matters but were largely excluded from senior decision-making positions. Following a government reshuffle and expansion in October 2013, the 39-member cabinet included six women, four of whom were junior ministers. The previous 31-member government included only one woman.

Several of the king's senior advisors were women. The 2011 elections saw an increase in the number of women in the Chamber of Representatives, from 34 to 67. A quota to provide women a position in the government produced 60 of those elected on a separate electoral list.

SECTION 4. CORRUPTION AND LACK OF TRANSPARENCY IN GOVERNMENT

The law provides criminal penalties for official corruption, but the government did not implement the law effectively. Officials often engaged in corrupt practices with impunity. Corruption was a serious problem in the executive branch, including police, as well as in the legislative and judicial branches. There were reports of mostly petty government corruption, but authorities investigated few cases and successfully prosecuted none during the year. In general observers considered corruption a serious problem, with insufficient governmental checks and balances to reduce its occurrence. Central Authority for the Prevention of Corruption (ICPC) head Abdessalam Aboudrar stated publicly in March that he was "still waiting for the power to conduct investigations," as he was not empowered to require institutions to respond to his organization's inquiries.

The king, who has made statements calling for judicial system reform since 2009, acknowledged the judiciary's lack of independence and susceptibility to influence. Many members of the well-entrenched and conservative judicial community were loath to adopt new procedures.

Corruption: The ICPC is responsible for combating corruption but lacked the necessary authority to require responses from government institutions. The agency noted the anticorruption situation had not improved significantly and that government policy continued to lack a strategic dimension and effective

government interlocutor with domestic and international NGOs, and interact with relevant UN bodies regarding international human rights obligations.

SECTION 6. DISCRIMINATION, SOCIETAL ABUSES, AND TRAFFICKING IN PERSONS

The constitution prohibits discrimination based on race, gender, disability, language, social status, faith, culture, regional origin, or any other personal circumstance. Discrimination occurred based on each of these factors. The 2011 constitution mandates the creation of a body to promote gender equality and resolve parity issues--the Authority for Equality and the Fight against All Forms of Discrimination -- but implementing legislation for the body had not been not adopted by year's end.

Women

Rape and Domestic Violence: The law punishes men convicted of rape with prison terms of five to 10 years; when the conviction involves a minor, the prison sentence ranges from 10 to 20 years. Spousal rape is not a crime. A sexual assault conviction may result in a prison sentence of up to one year and a fine of 15,000 dirhams ($1,800). Police were slow to act in domestic violence cases, and the government generally did not enforce the law. The vast majority of sexual assaults were not reported to police for social reasons; a 2010 government planning survey revealed that a victim's husband committed 55 percent of the acts of violence against women, and the wife reported it in only 3 percent of cases. Police selectively investigated cases; among the minority brought to trial, successful prosecutions were rare.

Domestic violence was widespread. Statistics on rape or sexual assault were unreliable due to underreporting. A Bureau of Statistics October 2013 planning publication, *The Moroccan Woman, by the Numbers*, revealed that 62.8 percent of women reported suffering an act of violence in the preceding year, although these figures were based on a 2009 survey. Various domestic advocacy groups, such as the Democratic League for Women's Rights, estimated that husbands perpetrated eight of 10 cases of violence against women.

On January 8, the *Official Bulletin* published an amended Article 475 of the family code implementing a change that disallowed rapists' exoneration through marriage to their victims. Previously rapists could avoid punishment by marrying the victim. Nonetheless, numerous articles of the penal code pertaining to rape perpetuate unequal treatment for women and provide insufficient protection, despite 2009 revisions to the family law.

The law does not specifically prohibit domestic violence against women, but the general prohibitions of the criminal code address such violence. By law high-level misdemeanors occur when a victim suffers injuries that result in 20 days of disability leave from work. Low-level misdemeanors occur when victims suffer disability for less than 20 days. According to NGOs, the courts rarely prosecuted perpetrators of low-level misdemeanors. Police generally treated domestic violence as a social rather than a criminal matter. Statistics provided by the government in October indicated that it provided direct support to 50 counseling centers for female victims of violence as part of a broader effort to support 659 projects benefitting women in society.

Physical abuse was legal grounds for divorce, although few women reported such abuse to authorities. Domestic violence mediation generally occurred within the family. Women choosing legal action generally preferred pursuing divorce in family courts rather than criminal prosecutions.

The law is lenient toward husbands who commit crimes against their wives. Police rarely became involved in domestic disputes. Several NGOs reported that laws were often unenforced due to societal pressures not to break up a family and to the conservative mentality of some police and court officials.

The government operated hotlines for victims of domestic violence. A small number of groups, such as the Antitrust Network and the Democratic League for Women's Rights, were also available to provide assistance and guidance to victims. Counseling centers existed exclusively in urban areas. Services for victims of violence in rural areas were generally limited to those provided by local police. Women's shelters were not government funded. A few NGOs made efforts to provide shelter for victims of domestic abuse. There were reports, however, that these shelters were not accessible to persons with disabilities. Courts had "victims of abuse cells" that brought together prosecutors, lawyers, judges, women's NGO representatives, and hospital personnel to review domestic and child abuse cases to provide for the best interests of women or children according to proper procedure.

Many domestic NGOs worked to advance women's rights and promote women's issues. Among these were the Democratic Association of Moroccan

Women, the Union for Women's Action, the Democratic League for Women's Rights, and the Moroccan Association for Women's Rights. All advocated enhanced political and civil rights for women. NGOs also promoted literacy and taught women basic hygiene, family planning, and childcare.

Female Genital Mutilation/Cutting (FGM/C): No law appears to prohibit FGM/C specifically, but there were no reports it occurred.

Sexual Harassment: Sexual harassment in the workplace is criminal only when it is an abuse of authority by a superior, as stipulated by the penal code. Violations are punishable by one to two years' imprisonment and a fine of 5,000 to 50,000 dirhams ($600 to $6,000). Authorities did not effectively enforce laws against sexual harassment. According to the government, although the law allows victims to sue employers, only a few did so. Most feared losing their job as a result or worried about proving the charge. NGOs reported widespread sexual harassment contributed to the low rate of female participation in the labor force. Government figures stated that "acts of violence committed in a place of work registered by the authorities" had dropped by 10.7 percent to 528 incidents, although the total number was extremely low and likely not representative of the real number of incidents in the country.

Reproductive Rights: Women generally were not discriminated against in accessing sexual and reproductive health care, including for sexually transmitted infections. Contraception is legal, and most forms were widely available. Individuals and couples have the right to attain the highest standard of reproductive health free from discrimination, coercion, and violence and the right to decide freely and responsibly the number, spacing, and timing of their children. Skilled health attendance at delivery and postpartum care were available for women who could afford it, with approximately 74 percent of overall births attended by skilled health personnel.

The most recent UN statistics showed there were approximately 100 maternal deaths per 100,000 live births in the country in 2010 and that 52 percent of women between the ages of 15 and 49 used a modern method of contraception in 2010. The major factors influencing maternal mortality and contraceptive prevalence rates were female illiteracy, lack of knowledge about availability of services, cost of services, social pressure against contraceptive use, and limited availability of transportation to health centers and hospitals for those in rural areas.

Discrimination: The constitution provides women equal rights in civil, political, economic, cultural, and environmental affairs. The law does not require equal pay for equal work.

Numerous problems related to discrimination against women remained. A Muslim woman's share of an inheritance, determined by sharia (Islamic law), varies depending on circumstances but is less than a man's. Under sharia, daughters receive half of what their brothers receive. If a woman is the only child, she receives half, and relatives receive the other half. A sole male heir would receive the entire estate. The 2004 reform of the family code did not change inheritance laws, which are not specifically addressed in the constitution.

According to the law, women are entitled to a one-third share of inherited property. While ministry decrees carry the force of law, implementation met considerable resistance from men in certain areas of the country. Despite lobbying by women's NGOs, enforcement of these property laws remained inconsistent. The Ministry of Interior further pressed for local enforcement of women's entitlement to collective land rights. A ministry circular published in 2012 requires all local authorities to follow the law rather than local customs, which in many regions allow male heirs to receive all lands. The government followed up with training for local authorities on the implementation of the land allocation process. Women's NGOs continued to press the government to codify women's rights in formal legislation.

The family code places the family under the joint responsibility of both spouses, makes divorce available by mutual consent, and places legal limits on polygamy. Implementation of family law reforms remained a problem. The judiciary lacked willingness to enforce them, as many judges did not agree with them. Corruption among working-level court clerks and lack of knowledge about its provisions among lawyers were also obstacles to enforcement of the law. Widespread female illiteracy also limited women's ability to navigate the legal system. The penal code criminalizes "knowingly hiding or subverting the search for a married woman who is evading the authority to which she is legally subject." This section was used to return women involuntarily to abusive homes.

There were few legal obstacles to women's participation in business and other economic activities. According to some entrepreneurs and NGOs, however, women experienced difficulty in accessing credit and owning and managing businesses. According to a 2011 government report, the rate of participation in the formal labor force for women was 25.5 percent. A 2012 study showed that women's wages on average were 15 percent below those of men.

The government led some efforts to improve the status of women in the workplace, most notably the 2011 constitution mandate for the creation of an Authority for Gender Parity and Fighting All Forms of Discrimination, an institution that was being developed jointly between the parliament and the CNDH. Article 19 of the constitution provides for the equal status of women in the realms of civics, politics, economics, social relations, culture, and the environment. The country participated in the Equal Futures Partnership, a multilateral initiative that encouraged member countries to empower women politically and economically.

Rural women faced restrictions for social and cultural reasons. Women were not represented in leadership positions in trade unions.

Children

Birth Registration: The law permits both parents to pass nationality to their children. There were, nonetheless, cases in which authorities denied identification papers to children because they were born to unmarried parents. In cases of undocumented children, NGOs, magistrates, and attorneys advocated for the children. The process of obtaining necessary identification papers was lengthy and arduous. According to press reports, during the year representatives of the Ministry of Interior refused to register the births of some children whose parents sought to give Amazigh names. Undocumented children could not register for school.

Education: Girls' representation in education in recent years improved significantly, especially in urban areas. According to a 2011 High Commission for Planning report, 26 percent of girls attended high school compared with 22 percent of boys; as of 2009-10, women accounted for 53 percent of those enrolled in higher education. In rural areas, however, progress was slow: 27 percent of girls did not attend school, compared with 19 percent of boys. In addition, according to 2011 UN statistics, 42 percent of women were illiterate. The government reported that 88 percent of the 769,402 persons who participated in literacy programs in 2012 were women.

Child Abuse: Although NGOs, human rights groups, media outlets, and the UN Children's Fund (UNICEF) claimed child abuse was widespread, there were no conclusive government statistics on the extent of the problem. Anecdotal evidence showed that abuse of child domestic servants was a problem. Prosecutions for child abuse were extremely rare. The Ministry of Youth and Sports managed 20 child protection centers, five specifically for girls. The centers were originally intended to provide an alternative to prison for underage delinquents, but were used to house delinquents, homeless children, victims of domestic violence, drug addicts, and other "children in distress" who had not committed a crime. Some centers housed minors convicted of homicide alongside minors who were victims of domestic abuse. This mingling of children in conflict with the law and children in distress also occurred during other stages of the process. While the budgets of the centers were low, conditions varied because some centers received charitable gifts.

Early and Forced Marriage: The legal age for marriage is 18, but parents, with informed consent of the minor, may secure a waiver from a judge for underage marriage. The judiciary approved the vast majority of petitions for underage marriages. In 2011 the Social Development Ministry reported there were more than 33,000 underage married girls. Child marriage remained a concern, especially in rural areas. UNICEF reported that 11 percent of women under the age of 20 were or had been married. According to the UN Population Fund's 2012 report, 16 percent of women between the ages of 20 and 24 had married before they were 18. No government efforts specifically focused on early marriage.

Female Genital Mutilation/Cutting (FGM/C): No law appears to prohibit FGM/C specifically, but there were no reports it occurred.

Sexual Exploitation of Children: The age of consent is 18. Penalties for sexual exploitation of children range from two years' to life imprisonment and fines from 9,550 dirhams ($1,160) to 344,000 dirhams ($41,700). Moreover, persons convicted of sexual exploitation may lose their national rights and right of residence for between five and 10 years. Convicted rapists and pedophiles are not eligible for pardons. Children were engaged in prostitution, and the country was a destination for sex tourism. The penal code also provides punishment for child pornography. Also see the Department of Labor's *Findings on the Worst Forms of Child Labor* at www.dol.gov/ilab/reports/child-labor/morocco.htm.

International Child Abductions: The country is a party to the 1980 Hague Convention on the Civil Aspects of International Child Abduction. For country-specific information see the Department of State's report at http://travel.state.gov/content/childabduction/english/country/morocco.html.

Anti-Semitism

Community leaders estimated the size of the Jewish population at approximately 4,000. Jews generally lived in safety, and the government provided them appropriate security. In July an assailant attacked a local rabbi in Casablanca, citing the Israeli military campaign in Gaza as the reason. The victim identified a suspect whom police took into custody. The outcome of this case was not published by year's end. Reports of anti-Semitic acts were rare.

TRAFFICKING IN PERSONS

See the Department of State's *Trafficking in Persons Report* at_www.state.gov/j/tip/rls/tiprpt/.

Persons with Disabilities

The law prohibits discrimination against persons with physical, sensory, intellectual, and mental disabilities in employment, education, and access to health care. The law also provides for regulations and building codes that ensure access for persons with disabilities. The government did not effectively enforce or implement these laws and regulations. While building codes enacted in 2003 require accessibility for all persons, the codes exempt most pre-2003 structures, and authorities rarely enforced them for new construction. Most public transportation was inaccessible to persons with disabilities, although the national rail system offered wheelchair ramps, handicap-accessible bathrooms, and special seating areas. Government policy provides that persons with disabilities should have equal access to information and communications. Special communication devices for the blind and deaf were not widely available.

The Ministry of Social Development, Family, and Solidarity has responsibility for protecting the rights of persons with disabilities and attempted to integrate persons with disabilities into society by implementing a quota of 7 percent for persons with disabilities in vocational training in the public sector and 5 percent in the private sector. Both sectors were far from achieving the quotas. The government maintained more than 400 integrated classes for children with learning disabilities, but integration was largely left to private charities. Families typically supported persons with disabilities, although some survived by begging.

National/Racial/Ethnic Minorities

Many of the poorest regions in the country, particularly the Middle Atlas region, were predominantly Amazigh and had illiteracy rates as high as 80 percent. Basic governmental services in this mountainous and underdeveloped region were not extensive. Official languages are Arabic and Amazigh, although Arabic predominates. French and Amazigh materials were available in the news media and, to a much lesser extent, educational institutions. Authorities made no progress toward passing a law to implement the constitutional provision making Amazigh an official language.

Approximately 60 percent of the population, including the royal family, claimed some Amazigh heritage. Amazigh cultural groups contended their traditions and language were rapidly being lost to Arabization. The government provided television programs in the three national Amazigh dialects of Tarifit, Tashelhit, and Tamazight. The government also offered Amazigh language classes in the curriculum of 5,151 schools. A lack of qualified teachers hindered otherwise expanding Amazigh language education. The palace-funded Royal Institute of Amazigh Culture created a university-level teacher-training program to eliminate the shortage of qualified teachers. Instruction in the Amazigh language is mandatory for students at the Ministry of Interior School for Administrators in Kenitra.

(See the Western Sahara report for information regarding discrimination against Sahrawis in Moroccan-controlled Western Sahara.)

Societal Abuses, Discrimination, and Acts of Violence Based on Sexual Orientation and Gender Identity

The penal code criminalizes consensual same-sex sexual activity with a maximum sentence of three years in prison. Questions of sexuality, sexual orientation, and gender identity were addressed in the media and in public more openly than in previous years.

Sexual orientation and gender identity constituted a basis for societal violence, harassment, blackmail, or other actions, generally at a local level, although with reduced frequency. There were infrequent reports of societal discrimination, physical violence, or harassment based on sexual orientation or gender identity. The government deems lesbian, gay, bisexual, or transgender (LGBT) orientation or identity illegal. Antidiscrimination laws do not apply to LGBT persons, and the penal code does not criminalize hate crimes. There was a stigma against LGBT persons, but there were no reports of discrimination based on sexual orientation or gender identity in employment, housing, access to education, or health care.

Authorities prosecuted individuals engaged in same-sex sexual activity at least once during the year. On July 2, an appellate court in Beni Mellal confirmed a judgment against six men who were convicted of homosexual acts in the city of Fqih Bensalah, 124 miles south of Rabat, after they were arrested in April. The court shortened the prison terms for two defendants and converted the sentences of the other four to suspended sentences.

HIV and AIDS Social Stigma

Persons living with HIV/AIDS faced discrimination and had limited treatment options. The Joint UN Program on HIV/AIDS reported that some health-care providers were reluctant to treat persons with HIV/AIDS due to fear of infection. There were domestic NGOs focused on treating HIV/AIDS patients.

SECTION 7. WORKER RIGHTS

a. Freedom of Association and the Right to Collective Bargaining

The constitution provides workers with the rights to form and join unions, strike, and bargain collectively, with some restrictions. The law prohibits certain categories of government employees, including members of the armed forces, police, and some members of the judiciary, from forming and joining unions and from conducting strikes. The law also excludes migrant workers from assuming leadership positions in unions. The labor code does not cover domestic workers.

According to the labor code, employer and worker representatives should conduct discussions to agree on the wages and employment conditions of unionized workers. The law allows several independent unions to exist, but the code requires 35 percent of the total employee base to be associated with a union for the union to be representative and able to engage in collective bargaining. The law prohibits antiunion discrimination and prohibits companies from dismissing workers for participating in legitimate union-organizing activities. Courts have the authority to reinstate workers dismissed arbitrarily and may enforce rulings that compel employers to pay damages and back pay.

The law concerning strikes requires compulsory arbitration of disputes, prohibits sit-ins, calls for a 10-day notice of a strike, and allows for the hiring of replacement workers. The government may intervene in strikes. A strike may not take place over matters covered in a collective contract for one year after the contract comes into force. The government has the authority to disperse strikers in public areas not authorized for demonstrations and to prevent the unauthorized occupancy of private space. Unions may neither engage in sabotage nor prevent those individuals who were not on strike from working.

The government did not adequately enforce labor laws due to a lack of inspection personnel and resources. Inspectors were also required to serve as mediators in disputes, requiring them to spend a significant amount of time in their offices, not conducting inspections. Enforcement procedures were subject to lengthy delays and appeals.

The government generally respected freedom of association and the right to collective bargaining. Employers limited the scope of collective bargaining, frequently setting wages unilaterally for the majority of unionized and nonunionized workers. Under the law unions are able to negotiate with the government on national-level labor issues. The government continued to prove unsuccessful in calling traditional tripartite social dialogue sessions, and none was held during the year. The last formal social dialogue session was called in 2012. At the sectoral level, trade unions negotiated with private employers concerning minimum wage, compensation, and other concerns.

Labor disputes were common and in some cases the result of employers failing to implement collective bargaining agreements and withholding wages. Trade unions complained that the government at times used Article 288 of the penal code to prosecute workers for striking and to suppress strikes, with the last such reported case in 2012, in Tangier, against maritime workers. Although most union federations were strongly allied with political parties, unions were generally free from government interference.

b. Prohibition of Forced or Compulsory Labor

The law prohibits all forms of forced or compulsory labor. The law penalizes forced labor of a worker by a fine for the first offense and a jail term of up to three months for subsequent offenses. Penalties for coerced child labor under the law range from one to three years' imprisonment. The legislation was not adequately enforced.

Domestic workers included certain vulnerable groups, such as migrant workers and children from rural areas. Domestic workers are not protected by labor laws, and certain migrant workers were subject to having their passports confiscated by employers and their wages withheld. Labor inspectors did not inspect small workshops and private homes where the majority of such practices occurred, as the law does not allow labor inspections in private homes. The effectiveness of inspectors was also limited by their small numbers, the broad geographic dispersion of sites, and scarce resources at their disposal.

Reports indicated that forced labor, especially of children, occurred. Some families from rural areas sent girls to work as maids in urban areas. Boys experienced forced labor as apprentices in the artisan and construction industries and in mechanic shops (see section 7.c.). Domestic NGOs reported that an undetermined number of Filipina domestic workers filed suits against their former employers for trafficking-like abuses, such as withholding passports or wages. Information on disposition of these cases was not available. Approximately 5,000 Filipinas were engaged in domestic work, some without employment contracts.

Also see the Department of State's Trafficking in Persons Report at www.state.gov/j/tip/rls/tiprpt/.

c. Prohibition of Child Labor and Minimum Age for Employment

The minimum age for employment in all sectors is 15. The law prohibits children younger than 16 from working more than 10 hours per day; employers must give them a break of at least one hour. The law does not permit children younger than 16 to work between the hours of 9 p.m. and 6 a.m. in nonagricultural work or between 8 p.m. and 5 a.m. in agriculture. The overwhelming majority of child laborers worked in rural agriculture, according to the government's statistical agency, the High Planning Commission. The law excludes seasonal agricultural work and work in traditional artisanal or handicraft sectors of business with fewer than five employees. The law prohibits employment of children younger than 18 in stone quarries, mines, or any other positions the government considers hazardous. The labor code, however, does not address domestic workers and therefore does not prohibit the employment of child maids or domestic workers.

The Ministry of Employment and Social Affairs is responsible for implementing and enforcing child labor laws and regulations. The law provides for legal sanctions against employers who recruit children under the age of 15, with fines ranging from 27,000 to 32,000 dirhams ($3,270 to $3,880). Punishment for violations of the child labor laws includes criminal penalties, civil fines, and withdrawal or suspension of one or more civil, national, or family rights, including denial of legal residence in the country for five to 10 years.

The ministry did not systematically enforce sanctions against child labor. According to various reports, police, prosecutors, and judges rarely enforced legal provisions on "forced labor in cases involving child domestics," and few parents of children working as domestics were willing or able to pursue legal avenues that were likely to provide any direct benefit.

Employers were successfully prosecuted throughout the year for employing a child domestic worker, but labor inspectors responsible for enforcing the labor code do not have jurisdiction to inspect private residences. The ministry's small cadre of labor inspectors did not monitor the informal sector. All 51 national labor inspectorates had an inspector trained in child labor issues and designated as a "focal point." These inspectors received up to 14 weeks of training from the International Labor Organization's (ILO's) International Program on the Elimination of Child Labor. During the year inspectors received additional training on respecting fundamental labor rights from the ILO.

Noncompliance with child labor laws was reported in agriculture and private urban residences, where parents sent children as young as six to work as domestic workers in urban areas, mainly Casablanca.

During the year the government launched a new "public integrated policy for the protection of children in Morocco" after a year-long review by an interministerial committee, chaired by the head of government. The Ministry of Solidarity, Women, Family, and Social Development has responsibility to oversee the plan and coordinate with other involved ministries. The plan is intended to incorporate lessons learned from the *2006-15 National Plan of Action for Children*, which it supplants. The plan includes six objectives:

integration of child protection into all policies and public programs; improvement of child protection laws; standardization of protective services; establishment of integrated regional child protection services; awareness campaigns and cultural training; and a monitoring and evaluation system.

The government expanded coordination with local, national, and international NGOs on education and training programs to combat child labor during the year. The Ministry of Employment and Social Affairs, led by the Office of the Director of Work in conjunction with NGOs, oversaw programs dealing with child labor. The programs sought to decrease the incidence of child labor by raising awareness of the problem, providing financial assistance to needy families, and lowering obstacles for at-risk children to attend school. In addition, the government made public education available to migrant children, lowering their vulnerability to child labor.

Child labor in rural areas in 2013 accounted for 88 percent of child workers, 94 percent of whom worked in agriculture, primarily on family farms. The Ministry of Employment and Social Affairs reported that, in the first trimester of the year (the most recent annualized inspection information available), focal-point inspectors conducted 312 visits, filed 1,201 reports, and issued 21 formal notices. The inspectors identified 357 child laborers, of whom 78 were under the age of 15. A total of 75 children under the age of 15 were removed from work, and 197 children between the ages of 15 and 17 were removed from hazardous work. There was no detailed information available on the collection of fines or on assistance to children identified through inspections.

Some children were apprenticed before the age of 12, particularly in small family-run workshops in the handicraft industry. Children also worked in the informal sector in textiles, light manufacturing, and carpet weaving. Children's safety and health conditions and wages were often substandard. The High Planning Commission reported approximately 10,000 children between the ages of seven and 15 worked in urban areas in 2013, largely in the service sector.

NGOs documented the physical and psychological abuse of children employed as domestic servants. Employers paid parents for their children's work. Most child domestics received food, lodging, and clothing instead of monetary compensation or were paid significantly below the minimum wage.

During the year the High Planning Commission reported a significant reduction in child labor over the past decade, claiming that during the year approximately 86,000 children between the ages of seven and 15 worked, compared with 517,000 children in the same age group in 1999.

Also see the Department of Labor's *Findings on the Worst Forms of Child Labor* at www.dol.gov/ilab/reports/child-labor/morocco.htm.

d. Discrimination with Respect to Employment or Occupation

Article 9 of the labor code prohibits companies from adopting "with regard to employees, any discrimination based on race, color, gender, handicap, marital status, religion, political opinion, trade union affiliation, national ancestry, or social origin, resulting in a violation or alteration of the principle of equal opportunity or treatment on equal footing as regards employment or the practice of a profession, in particular with regard to recruitment, conduct and labor distribution, vocational training, wage, advances, the granting of social benefits, disciplinary measures and dismissal." Article 12 of the code describes the sanctions for violations of Article 9. Furthermore, Article 346 states: "Any discrimination with relation to wage between the two sexes for work of equal value is prohibited." The law does not address sexual orientation or gender identity in this context. The law prohibits the employment of women and youths (between the ages of 15 and 17) in certain occupations that are considered hazardous, such as mines. Discrimination in all categories prohibited by law occurred, as the government lacked sufficient human and financial resources to effectively enforce these laws. Migrant worker organizations reported that some migrants experienced discrimination in hiring, wages, or conditions of employment, although the regularization campaign during the year provided thousands of formerly undocumented migrant workers with residency cards to improve their employment opportunities and provide protections for this otherwise vulnerable population.

e. Acceptable Conditions of Work

The minimum wage was 97 dirhams ($11.70) per day in the industrialized sector and 63 dirhams ($7.20) per day for agricultural workers. The World Bank absolute poverty-level threshold wage was 70 dirhams ($8.50) per day. Including traditional holiday-related bonuses, workers generally received the equivalent of 13 to 16 months' salary each year. Informal businesses employed approximately 60 percent of the labor force and often ignored minimum wage requirements. A temporary contract program (Contracts Anapac) designed to help new entrants into the job market denied young workers many social protections, enabled long working hours, and paid below the minimum wage. The program was also subject to abuse, replacing full time workers with temporary workers.

The law provides for a 44- to 48-hour maximum workweek with no more than 10 hours in a single day, premium pay for overtime, paid public and annual holidays, and minimum conditions for health and safety, including a prohibition on night work for women and minors. The law prohibits excessive overtime. The labor code does not cover domestic workers, who were primarily female citizens. Filipina domestic workers openly complained of sexual exploitation from abusive employers, who frequently confiscated their passports and paid them salaries of less than 2,500 dirhams ($300) per month.

Occupational health and safety standards, reviewed and enforced by the Ministry of Employment and Social Affairs, are rudimentary, except for a prohibition on the employment of women and children in certain dangerous occupations. The law prohibits persons under the age of 18 from hazardous work in 33 areas, including working in mines, handling dangerous materials, transporting explosives, and operating heavy machinery.

Many employers did not observe the legal provisions for conditions of work. The government did not effectively enforce basic provisions of the labor code, such as payment of the minimum wage and other basic benefits under the National Social Security Fund. The country's labor inspectors attempted to monitor working conditions and investigate accidents, but lack of resources prevented effective enforcement of labor laws. Penalties were generally not sufficient to deter violations.

According to NGOs, no major workplace accidents occurred during the year; however, there were numerous media reports of accidents, sometimes fatal, on construction sites that had substandard standards or lacked safety equipment. In the formal sector, workers can remove themselves from situations that endangered health or safety without jeopardy to their employment and authorities effectively protected employees in this situation.

In: Morocco
Editor: Wilson Graves

ISBN: 978-1-63485-107-7

Chapter 4

MORROCCO 2014 INTERNATIONAL RELIGIOUS FREEDOM REPORT*

U.S. Department of State; Bureau of Democracy, Human Rights and Labor

EXECUTIVE SUMMARY

The constitution stipulates that Morocco is a sovereign Muslim state and Islam is the religion of the state. It prohibits political parties, parliamentarians, and constitutional amendments from attempting to infringe upon Islam. The constitution guarantees the freedom of thought and practice of one's religious affairs. The criminal code prohibits efforts by non-Muslims to proselytize, and the government discouraged conversion from Islam. The Ministry of Endowments and Islamic Affairs (MEIA) controls the content of preaching in mosques, religious education, and broadcast religious material. The government allows foreign Christian communities to attend worship services in approved places, although Christian citizens generally do not attend these services. There are no known Shia mosques or Bahai houses of worship. The government continued to restrict the distribution of non-Islamic religious materials, as well as some Islamic materials that it deemed inconsistent with the Maliki-Ashari school of Sunni Islam. The government monitored the

* Citation Note: This is an edited, reformatted and augmented version of a report issued by the U.S. Department of State; Bureau of Democracy, Human Rights and Labor, October 2015.

activities of religious groups and placed restrictions on individuals and groups when it deemed their actions exceeded the bounds of acceptable religious or political activity.

There were reports of anti-Semitism, although most Jews live in safety throughout the country. Christian citizens reported official harassment and pressure to convert from non-Christian family and friends. Most members of the Shia and Bahai communities avoided disclosing their religious affiliation.

The Ambassador, embassy and consulate general officers, and other U.S. government officials discussed religious freedom with the government within the context of official visits and on other occasions. The bilateral strategic dialogue promoted religious tolerance. The Assistant Secretary of State for Educational and Cultural Affairs led a working group focusing on interfaith dialogue and youth. The U.S. government sponsored programs focused on religious tolerance and dialogue.

Section I. Religious Demography

The U.S. government estimates the population at 33 million (July 2014 estimate). More than 99 percent is Sunni Muslim. Groups together constituting less than 1 percent of the population include Christians, Jews, Shia Muslims, and Bahais. According to Jewish community leaders, there are an estimated 3,000 to 4,000 Jews, approximately 2,500 of whom reside in Casablanca. The Rabat and Marrakech Jewish communities each have approximately 100 members.

The predominantly Roman Catholic and Protestant foreign resident Christian community consists of approximately 5,000 members, although some clergy estimate the number to be as high as 25,000. Most foreign resident Christians live in the Casablanca, Tangier, and Rabat urban areas. The Protestant community includes the French Protestant community (Evangelical Church of Morocco (EEM, its French acronym)); the Moroccan Association of Protestant Churches (AMEP, its French acronym), a network of autonomous, generally English-speaking foreign resident communities; and Anglican churches in Casablanca and Tangier. There is a Russian Orthodox church in Rabat and a Greek Orthodox church in Casablanca. Various local Christian leaders estimate that there are 4,000 to 8,000 citizen Christians (mostly ethnic Amazigh) who attend "house" churches and live predominantly in the south.

There are an estimated 3,000 to 8,000 Shia Muslims, most of them foreign residents from Lebanon, Syria, or Iraq, but including a small number of citizens. There are 350-400 Bahais in urban areas, particularly in Tangier. There are no known Shia mosques or Bahai houses of worship.

Section II. Status of Government Respect for Religious Freedom

Legal Framework

The constitution stipulates that Morocco is a sovereign Muslim state and Islam is the religion of the state. It prohibits political parties, parliamentarians, or constitutional amendments from attempting to infringe upon Islam. The constitution guarantees the freedom of thought and practice of one's religious affairs. The constitution stipulates that the king hold the Islamic title of Commander of the Faithful, protector of Islam, and the guarantor of freedom of worship in the country. According to the constitution, only the High Council of Ulema, a group headed and appointed by the king with representatives from all regions of the country, may issue scholarly fatwas (formal religious opinions), which become binding only through endorsement by the king in a royal decree.

The criminal code prohibits attempts by non-Muslims to "shake the faith" of Moroccans from the Maliki-Ashari school of Islam, which the government has interpreted to mean attempting to convert Muslims to other religions. Restricted activities include the distribution of non-Islamic religious materials. By law, impeding or preventing one or more persons from worshipping or from attending worship services of any religion may be punished by six months to three years of imprisonment and a fine of 115 to 575 dirhams ($13 to $64). The law applies the same penalty to "anyone who employs enticements to undermine the faith of a Muslim or to convert him to another religion." It also provides the right to a court trial for anyone accused of such an offense. Voluntary conversion is not a crime under the criminal or civil codes.

The law permits the government to expel summarily any non-citizen resident it determines to be "a threat to public order," even where other laws require due process first. The government has cited this law to expel or refuse entry to foreign Christians accused or suspected of proselytizing.

The law requires non-Maliki-Ashari Muslim and non-Jewish religious groups to register before they are able to undertake financial transactions or conduct other business as private associations and legal entities. The registration requirements for religious organizations are the same as all other associations. Registered churches and associations include the Roman

Catholic, Russian Orthodox, Greek Orthodox, French Protestant, and Anglican Churches. These churches existed before independence in 1956 and operate within an officially recognized organization, the Council of Christian Churches of Morocco (CECM by its French acronym). The government recognizes foreign resident Protestant churches that do not fall under the CECM but formed under the auspices of AMEP. The government currently does not recognize Bahai or Shia as registered religious organizations.

There is a separate set of laws and courts with authority over personal status matters for Jews, covering issues such as marriage, inheritance, and other family matters. Rabbinical authorities, who are also court officials, administer Jewish family courts. Muslim judges trained in the country's interpretation of sharia administer the courts for personal status matters for all other religious groups. Christians, however, inherit according to civil law. There are no legal mechanisms recognizing the Christian community (or other non-Muslims) in the same way the state recognizes the Jewish community. Non-Muslims must formally convert to Islam and be a permanent resident before they can become guardians of abandoned or orphaned children. According to the law, a Muslim man may marry a non-Muslim woman, but a Muslim woman may not marry a non-Muslim man unless he converts to Islam.

The constitution and the law governing the media sector prohibit any citizen, including members of parliament normally immune from arrest, from criticizing Islam. Such expressions are punishable by imprisonment. The High Authority for Audiovisual Communications requires all eight television stations to dedicate 5 percent of their airtime to religious content. All public channels are required to broadcast the Islamic call to prayer five times daily.

The penal code states that any person known to be Muslim who breaks the fast in public during the month of Ramadan without an exception granted by religious authorities is liable for punishment of six months in prison and a fine of 200 to 500 dirhams ($22 to $55).

The constitution prohibits political parties founded on religious, ethnic, linguistic, or regional bases. The government permits several parties identified as "Islamically-oriented" rather than Islamist, and some have attracted substantial support, including the Party of Justice and Development (PJD), which is the largest political party in parliament and leads the current coalition government.

The constitution guarantees civil society organizations can constitute and exercise their activities in freedom, within the scope of respect for the constitution. The law on associations states that any association that seeks to undermine the monarchy, Islam, or the country's territorial integrity is invalid. Groups must register with the interior ministry, which can deny a registration based on the group's ideology. For example, the government does not recognize the Justice and Charity Organization (JCO), which rejects the preeminence of the king's spiritual authority.

The MEIA must authorize the construction of new mosques, even those constructed using private funds.

Legal provisions provide tax benefits, land and building grants, subsidies, and customs exemptions for imports necessary for the religious activities of Muslims, Jews, and foreign resident Christians.

There is no law requiring the designation of religion on passports or national identity documents. There are no prohibitions on religious clothing or symbols in either the public or private sphere.

By law, all educational institutions must teach Sunni Islam in accordance with the teachings of the Maliki-Ashari school. The government's annual education budget funds the teaching of Islam in all public schools and Judaism in some public schools. Foreign-run schools, such as the French and Spanish schools, have the option of not including any religious instruction within the school's curriculum. Private Jewish schools are able to teach Judaism.

Government Practices

The government reportedly arrested and deported an individual on accusations of proselytizing Muslims. The government discouraged conversion from Islam and continued to restrict the distribution of non-Islamic religious materials, as well as some Islamic materials that it deemed inconsistent with the Maliki-Ashari school of Sunni Islam. Several individuals were arrested and sentenced for eating or drinking alcohol in public during the Ramadan fast. Government institutions, such as the MEIA and security services, monitored, and in some cases, restricted activities of Muslims and non-Muslims.

In February media reported that a U.S. citizen legally resident in the country for more than a decade had been arrested on allegations of Christian proselytizing in Al Hoceima. According to media reports, the individual was paying teenage girls to translate Christian materials into Tamazight (Berber) and Arabic, and police found him in possession of proselytizing materials. While media reported that authorities deported the individual to Melilla following a complaint by a neighboring Muslim cleric, the foreign ministry stated he was not arrested but “taken into protective custody” because neighborhood residents were threatening him with violence. The U.S. citizen departed the country without prosecution.

Also in February a court of appeals in Fez dismissed a charge against Mohammed El Baldi, a Moroccan convert to Christianity, on the grounds of lack of evidence. El Baldi had been arrested in 2013 for proselytizing to minors in Taounate and sentenced to two-and-a-half years in prison and a fine of 5000 dirhams ($554).

In July five individuals were arrested in Souk El Arbaa for drinking alcohol and eating in public during Ramadan. They received the maximum sentence of six months in prison. Authorities made another arrest in July in Tiznit of an individual seen eating in public during Ramadan. The Tiznit case led to a sentence of five months in prison.

In September the government permitted its appointed caretaker to permanently resettle the approximately 30 remaining children from the Village of Hope (VOH) orphanage in Ain Leuhto to a center in Meknes acceptable to the foreign resident Christians involved with the VOH. The ultimate disposition of the children had not been settled since 2010, when the government expelled or declared persona non-grata, on accusations of proselytizing, seven foreign families who operated the VOH.

Foreigners attended religious services without restriction at places of worship belonging to officially recognized Catholic, Orthodox, or Protestant Churches. Foreign-resident Christian church officials, however, reported that Moroccan Christians rarely attended their churches, and they did not encourage them to do so to avoid accusations of proselytizing. Fears of government surveillance led most Christian, Bahai, and Shia to refrain from public worship; most met discreetly in their members’ homes. Local Christians stated the authorities made phone or house calls several times a year to demonstrate they had lists of members of Christian networks and monitored Christian activities. Some Christian citizens reported authorities pressured Christian converts to renounce their faith by informing the converts’ friends, relatives, and employers of the individuals’ conversion.

The government continued to fund the study of Jewish culture and its artistic, literary, and scientific heritage at some universities. At the University of Rabat, Hebrew and comparative religion were taught in the Department of Islamic Studies. The monarchy also continued to support the rehabilitation of synagogues throughout the country, an effort it stated it deemed necessary to preserve the country’s religious and cultural heritage and to serve as a symbol of tolerance.

The government permitted the display and sale of Bibles in French, English, and Spanish. A limited number of Arabic translations of the Bible were available for sale in a few bookshops, but authorities often confiscated Bibles they believed were intended for proselytizing. The government did not allow the free public distribution of non-Sunni Muslim religious materials.

The government generally tolerated activities limited to the propagation of Sunni Islam, education, and charity. For example, the Unity and Reform Movement, the PJD's social and religious outreach branch, operated without special restrictions. At times, the government suppressed the activities of politically active religious groups, such as the banned yet tolerated JCO. The JCO continued to organize through participation in political demonstrations and the management of internet sites, although the government occasionally prevented the organization's meetings and restricted public distribution of the JCO's published materials. The government monitored the activities of mosques and non-Muslim religious groups, and placed some restrictions on members of religious groups when it deemed their actions exceeded the bounds of acceptable religious or political activity. In February, for example, Salafi cleric Abu Naim was convicted of defamation and insulting a political figure when he pronounced *takfir* (anathematization) upon a prominent politician and vehemently denounced the political left, secularists, and certain media outlets.

The MEIA was the principal institution responsible for shaping the country's religious sphere and promoting its interpretation of Sunni Islam valuing moderation and tolerance. The MEIA provided guidance to imams and monitored Friday mosque sermons and Quranic schools to prevent what the ministry considered inflammatory or extremist rhetoric and to ensure that teaching followed approved doctrine. The ministry tried to control the sale of what it considered extremist books, videotapes, and DVDs. The government required that mosques close to the public shortly after daily prayer times to prevent use of the premises for unauthorized activity.

Broadcast media covered prominently the government's efforts to disseminate information about Islam over dedicated state-funded Quranic television and radio channels. The television channel *Assadissa* (*Sixth*) continued to function as a partnership between three governmental entities: the National Society for Radio and Television, the communications ministry, and the MEIA. Programming consisted primarily of Quran and *hadith* (traditional teachings) readings and exegesis, although it also covered health, family, youth, and social issues, highlighting the government's interpretation of Islam in traditions and practice of the Islamic legacy. It broadcast this programming in Arabic and French, as well as in Amazigh (Berber) and Hassani (Saharan dialect).

The MEIA continued to employ over 500 chief imams and over 200 female Muslim spiritual guides (*murshidat*), who taught religious subjects, provided counsel on a variety of matters, including women's legal rights and family planning, and managed programs in which men participate; however, the *murshidat* did not deliver Friday sermons in mosques or lead group prayers.

In May the king broke ground on a new royal regional imam training institute as part of a royal initiative to promote openness and tolerance among the new generation of male and female spiritual guides. Al Akhawayn University in Ifrane, a royally-sponsored university, continued to offer an advanced degree in Islamic studies with an emphasis in comparative religion, including a mastery of Greek and Hebrew, to MEIA-nominated imams and others.

Section III. Status of Societal Respect for Religious Freedom

There were isolated reports of public anti-Semitism, and some Moroccan Christians reported the government did not respond to continued societal harassment. Fears of societal harassment led many non-Maliki-Ashari Muslims and non-Jewish groups to practice their faiths discreetly.

In February the Mimouna Jewish student group at Al Akhawayn University in Ifrane launched a Moroccan Jewish caravan that visited college campuses in major cities throughout the country to promote Judeo-Moroccan culture and religious tolerance.

In February the Simon Wiesenthal Center, a Jewish-American organization, publicly denounced the presence of anti-Semitic literature at an annual book fair in Casablanca. There was no indication the government promoted the literature.

In June a group of citizen human rights activists founded the Moroccan Observatory to Fight Anti-Semitism after a group of citizens sparked controversy by cancelling their visit to a Tel Aviv University annex. The founders said the group would seek to strengthen ties between citizens residing in the country and those residing in Israel, and to inform citizens objectively about the Israeli-Palestinian conflict.

In July a man attacked a rabbi walking to his synagogue in Casablanca, allegedly in response to the conflict in Gaza. Several days later, the same individual was reported for throwing stones at another Jewish citizen. The authorities soon apprehended the individual. In November he was sentenced to 10 months in prison and a fine of 1000 dirhams ($111). The court acquitted him of any anti-Semitism charges.

Traditionally, Muslims in the country have characterized the Bahai Faith as a heretical deviation from Islam and consequently considered Bahais apostates.

Most members of the Shia and Bahai communities avoided disclosing their religious affiliation.

Some female citizens stated it was difficult to find employment in professional sectors – including business and education, or with the army or police – if they wore a hijab, reporting that some employers either encouraged or required women to remove their headscarves during working hours.

In general, Jewish citizens attended services at synagogues and lived in safety throughout the country. Annual Jewish commemorations took place and Jewish visitors regularly visited religious sites. Muslim citizens studied at Christian and Jewish public and private schools. Muslim students constituted the majority at Jewish schools in Casablanca, and a Jewish community hospital provided care to low-income citizens regardless of religion. Jews served in high-level government positions including as a royal advisor and an ambassador-at-large to represent religious diversity and tolerance.

Section IV. U.S. Government Policy

The U.S. government promoted religious tolerance in the bilateral strategic dialogue. The Assistant Secretary of State for Educational and Cultural Affairs led a working group that discussed interfaith dialogue and youth. The working group sponsored a joint international conference on women in monotheistic religions held in Rabat in November. The Ambassador, embassy and consulate general officers, and visiting U.S. government officials including the U.S. Special Envoy to the Organization of Islamic Cooperation, met with senior government and religious officials, including in the MEIA, as well as with Muslim religious scholars, leaders of the Jewish community, Christian foreign residents, leaders of registered and unregistered Christian groups, and other local religious groups to promote religious freedom. The U.S. government sponsored programs focused on religious tolerance and freedom. During Ramadan, the Ambassador hosted an interfaith iftar for Moroccan and visiting U.S. religious leaders.

In: Morocco
Editor: Wilson Graves

ISBN: 978-1-63485-107-7

Chapter 5

MOROCCO INVESTMENT CLIMATE STATEMENT 2015*

Bureau of Economic and Business Affairs

EXECUTIVE SUMMARY

Despite global economic uncertainty and slowed capital inflows into North Africa following the regional upheaval linked to the Arab Spring, the Moroccan government is making great strides in attracting foreign direct investment (FDI) to the country. It actively encourages foreign investment and has sought to facilitate it through macro-economic policies, trade liberalization, and structural reforms. Further, due to its political stability, solid infrastructure, and strategic location, Morocco is rapidly becoming a regional manufacturing and export base for international companies. Morocco's overarching economic development plan is based on leveraging its location, along the Strait of Gibraltar between Spain and Africa, to transform the country into a regional hub for North, West, and Sub-Saharan Africa for shipping, logistics, finance, manufacturing, assembly, and sales.

The Government of Morocco has implemented a series of sector strategies aimed at raising performance and output in key revenue-earning sectors, boosting employment, and attracting foreign investment. Notably, its 2009 National Plan for Industrial Development set the groundwork for large-scale

* This is an edited, reformatted and augmented version of a report issued by the U.S. Department of State, June 2015.

global investments, such as those by France's Renault in Tangier and Canada's Bombardier in Casablanca. The strategy focuses on developing export-oriented economic sectors (aeronautics, automotive, offshoring, and electronics) and contributed roughly 75,000 jobs to the manufacturing sector in the past ten years. In 2014, the government refreshed its industrial strategy which aims to amplify the impacts of its 2009 plan, accelerating job creation and growth in the industrial sector, largely by attracting FDI and strengthening the linkages between the small business sector and the Morocco's industrial leaders. The ambitious 2014 strategy aims to create 500,000 new jobs in manufacturing by 2020. In addition to its industrial strategy, the Casablanca Finance City (CFC), Morocco's flagship project launched in 2010 by King Mohammed VI, aims to make Casablanca a financial hub for Africa, offering incentives for firms who locate their regional headquarters in the financial and business center.

Morocco has ratified 62 bilateral agreements for the promotion and protection of investments and 51 agreements that aim to eliminate the double taxation of income or gains. Its Investment Charter has put in place a convertibility system for foreign investors and gives investors the freedom to transfer profits. Morocco's Free Trade Agreement (FTA) with the United States entered into force in 2006. Since then, overall bilateral trade has increased by more than 300 percent.

Multinational companies cite Morocco's security and stability as positive factors contributing to the country's appeal as a base for regional activities. Despite significant progress in its business and economic environment, they also express concern over Morocco's lack of skilled labor, weak intellectual property rights protection, and the lack of regulatory transparency. Nevertheless, foreign companies operating in Morocco still find it suitably profitable to maintain their presence.

1. Openness to, and Restrictions Upon, Foreign Investment
Attitude toward Foreign Direct Investment

Morocco actively encourages foreign investment and has sought to facilitate it through macroeconomic policies, trade liberalization, structural reforms, as well as investments in infrastructure and incentives for investors. As it works to position itself as a gateway to Africa, multinational companies are beginning to relocate their regional headquarters to Morocco. In 2012, Morocco became the first Middle East and North Africa partner to endorse the

Joint Principles for International Investment and the Joint Principles for Information and Communication Technology (ICT) Services, sending a strong signal to domestic and international investors that Morocco embraces an open, 21st century approach to investment and growth. Despite its general openness to FDI, the government generally requires investors to use domestic content in goods or technologies, and some government originated tenders have local content requirements, particularly in certain sectors.

Under the U.S.-Morocco Free Trade Agreement (FTA) and the Association Agreement with the European Union (EU), Morocco has eliminated or reduced its tariffs on imports from the U.S. and the EU. Morocco has also signed a quadrilateral FTA with Tunisia, Egypt and Jordan (under the Agadir Declaration), an FTA with Turkey, and concluded third round FTA talks with Canada in June 2012. In 2008, Morocco was the first country in the region to be granted "advanced status" with the EU. In April 2014, Morocco entered into fourth round talks with the EU for a Deep and Comprehensive FTA. Additionally, Morocco is seeking various bilateral memorandum of understandings with African, Asian and Latin American countries in an effort to expand trade and investment in targeted sectors. However, the Moroccan government has put on hold negotiations for new FTAs while it assesses the benefits it has received thus far from its current agreements.

In September 2012, the U.S. and Morocco launched a Strategic Dialogue, annual high level consultations that promote mutual priorities including efforts to increase trade and investment. Further, the annual U.S.-Morocco Business Development Conference (BDC) provides a platform to strengthen business-to-business ties.

Morocco is ranked 71 out of 189 economies in the 2015 Doing Business report, three positions lower than in 2014, as a result of the increased challenges associated with starting a business, paying taxes, resolving insolvency issues, minority investor protection, and obtaining credit. However, registering property and trading across borders improved over the course of the year, despite the fact that Morocco still lags far behind the region with respect to the former category.

Other Investment Policy Reviews

UNCTAD's 2008 Investment Policy Review of Morocco can be found here (French and Spanish): http://unctad.org/en/pages/PublicationArchive.aspx?publicationid=9321 The Investment Policy Review noted that Morocco had the potential to attract increased FDI inflows and FDI of a high quality in order to meet the development objective of the "Plan Emergence" of moving into high value added activities. UNCTAD analyzes investment conditions and opportunities in Morocco in a 2010 report available here (French): http://unctad.org/fr/Docs/diaepcb20093_fr.pdf.

The World Trade Organization (WTO) 2009 Trade Policy Review (TPR) of Morocco can be found here: http://www.wto.org/english/tratop_e/tpr_e/tp317_e.htm. The review found that the macroeconomic and structural reforms, including trade reforms, pursued by Morocco since the previous TPR (2003) have contributed to the growth diversification and positive overall performance of its economy.

The OECD's 2010 Investment Policy Review of Morocco can be found here: http://www.oecd.org/daf/inv/internationalinvestmentagreements/morocco-investmentpolicyreview-oecd.htm. The review found that Morocco has adopted a series of laws and amendments needed to improve the local investment climate. Progress has been made in improving transparency and business access to information, and in reducing the time and cost of administrative procedures.

Laws/Regulations of Foreign Direct Investment

Law 18-95 of October 1995, constituting the Investment Charter, (http://www.usamorocco.org/Charte.htm) is the principal Moroccan text concerning investment and applies to both domestic and foreign investment.

The Foreign Exchange Office's Circular 1589 of September 1992 instituted a convertibility regime that allows foreign investors to conduct their investment operations in Morocco freely. The 1995 Charter guarantees free transfer of funds (Article 16) and gives foreign investors the freedom to transfer profits and capital for persons who make investments in foreign currency (Article 15).

Morocco accepted Article VIII of the Articles of Agreement of the International Monetary Fund in January 1993.

Further information about Morocco's investment laws and procedures is available on the Invest in Morocco website at: http://www.doingbusiness.org/data/exploreeconomies/morocco/

Industrial Promotion

Building on its previous industrial development strategy, in 2014 Morocco introduced an ambitious seven-year industrial growth and acceleration plan. It allocates USD 2.1 billion to a public industrial investment fund to support programs that will increase manufacturing's share of GDP from 14 to 23 percent and to create 500,000 new jobs by 2020. The plan aims to support the development of small and medium-sized enterprises (SMEs), improve youth employability, support integrated industrial platforms, and promote exports, using increased foreign investment to boost knowledge sharing and technology transfer. At the same time, it aims to protect local industries against 'unfair' competition and reduce import dependency. The plan targets the same sectors as its predecessor, including automotive, aeronautics, offshoring, electronics, textile and leather, and the food industry.

More information on the Industrial Acceleration Plan can be found here: http://www.invest.gov.ma/?Id=23&lang=en.

Morocco's 2009 National Plan for Industrial Development set the groundwork for large-scale global investments, such as those by France's Renault in Tangier and Canada's Bombardier in Casablanca. The strategy focused on developing export-oriented economic sectors in which Morocco had a comparative advantage, including four that had attracted significant FDI – automobile, aeronautics, electronics, and offshoring – and three that were largely financed by domestic investment – leather, food processing, and textiles. The plan also developed Morocco's industrial parks, offering investors land for new or expanding businesses, special tax breaks, transport connections, and services such as security, telecommunications, and recruitment support. In the past ten years, the manufacturing sector created 75,000 jobs.

More information on this strategy can be found here: http://www.emergence.gov.ma/en/Pacte/Pages/LePacte.aspx.

The Moroccan government established the CFC in December 2010 to position Casablanca as a financial hub for Francophone Africa. The CFC exclusively targets financial institutions (investment banks, asset management firms, private equity firms, and insurance companies), multinational regional headquarters, and professional services firms (consulting, law, audit, and credit rating agencies). The CFC is ranked 42 of 83 worldwide per the March 2015 Global Financial Centers Index, which represents a 21-position improvement over the March 2014 ranking. The CFC is the second ranked financial center in Africa, after Johannesburg.

By 2020, Morocco plans to have invested USD18.95 billion in its Energy Strategy to decrease energy dependence, preserve the environment, and generate 50,000 jobs. Its goal is to have 42 percent of its total electrical power produced by renewable energy (solar, wind, and hydraulic). With a goal to make solar energy 14 percent of total electric capacity, Morocco aims to increase solar electric production capacity to 2000 MW by 2020 principally using two technologies: concentrated solar power and photovoltaic. It plans to increase installed wind-generated electrical capacity from 280 MW in 2010 to 2000 MW by 2020, reducing CO2 emissions by 5.6 million tons per year. In addition, Morocco recently announced plans to invest $4.6 billion in an LNG regasification terminal and related infrastructure, including several gas to power plants, to increase its use of natural gas for the production of electricity.

Morocco has 13 commercial ports that processed 2.5 million twenty-foot-container equivalent units in 2013, according to the World Bank. Morocco has two port management agencies, the National Port Agency (ANP) and Tanger-Med Special Agency (TMSA). TMSA manages Tanger Med, the largest port by volume in Morocco. Tanger-Med Port terminals 1 and 2 are operational and traffic has now reached capacity, exceeding 3 million containers in 2014, which represented a 20 percent increase over 2013. The port is expected to process 8 million containers, 7 million passengers, 700,000 trucks, 2 million vehicles, and 10 million MT. Once fully operational in 2016, Tanger Med is expected to rank as the largest transshipment hub in Africa.

Morocco has implemented other sector strategies including the Green Morocco Plan (to revive Morocco's agriculture sector), Digital Morocco 2013 Plan (to position Morocco as a dynamic emerging country in information technology), Halieutis Plan (to improve the competitiveness of Morocco's fishing industry), Logistics Strategy (to improve logistic services and transportation infrastructure), National Strategy for the Craft Industry (to promote production and sales of handicrafts), and Tourism Vision 2020 strategy (to double the number of foreign tourists and triple the number of national domestic travelers). To support the tourism strategy, the government is implementing a development strategy to promote Casablanca airport as an international hub for traffic to Central and West Africa, and develop Marrakech airport as a hub for African traffic toward Europe. It also seeks to improve Morocco's airport infrastructure through airport extension, modernization, and new construction.

Morocco's main platform for information about investing in the country is Invest in Morocco or the Moroccan Investment Development Agency (AMDI). Information on its services as well as investing in Morocco can be found at: http://www.invest.gov.ma/?Id=1&lang=en.

Limits on Foreign Control

According to the OECD 2010 Investment Policy Review, Morocco places limits on foreign investment in air and maritime transport companies and maritime fisheries, allowing for only a minority stake (49 percent or less for air transport and 25 percent or less for maritime and fishing vessels). Although foreigners are prohibited from owning and cultivating agricultural land, they can purchase it for non-agricultural purposes. Morocco has sought to encourage foreign investment in the agricultural sector by making land available to foreigners through leases of up to 99 years. French, Spanish and Middle Eastern investment in the sector centers mostly on citrus and olives, with smaller investment in grapes and berries.

Morocco adheres to the OECD Declaration on International Investment and Multinational Enterprises. Morocco's OECD FDI Regulatory Restrictiveness Index in 2010 was 0.067 (closed economy = 1; open = 0). http://www.oecd.org/daf/inv/internationalinvestmentagreements/45563285.pdf.

Privatization Program

Foreign investors are permitted to participate in privatization programs. In 1993, an ambitious program of privatization was initiated, focused on key sectors such as telecommunications, agribusiness, banking, and tourism, among others. When it ended in August 2011, total revenue from divestment in state-owned enterprise (SOE) and the granting of telecom licenses totaled about 107 billion dirhams (approximately USD13 billion). Privatization has attracted FDI, giving a boost to Morocco's economy.

Screening of FDI

The formalities related to investing in Morocco do not pose a meaningful barrier to investment in the country. The U.S. Mission is not aware of any formal investment review process or any instances in which investors have been turned away.

Competition Law

Restrictive agreements and practices are regulated by the Competition Law. Morocco's Competition Law no. 06-99 on Free Pricing and Competition (June 2000) outlines the authority of the Competition Council (http://conseil-concurrence.ma/) as an independent executive body with investigatory powers. Together with the Central Authority for the Prevention of Corruption, the Competition Council is one of the main actors in charge of improving public governance and advocating for further market liberalization.

Investment Trends

Morocco's investment trend rankings generally improved in 2014.

Table 1.

Measure	Year	Index or Rank	Website Address
TI Corruption Perceptions index	2014	80 of 175	transparency.org/cpi2014/results
World Bank's Doing Business Report "Ease of Doing Business"	2015	71 or 189	doingbusiness.org/rankings
Global Innovation Index	2014	84 of 143	globalinnovationindex.org/content.aspx?page=data-analysis
World Bank GNI per capita	2013	USD 3,020	data.worldbank.org/indicator/NY.GNP.PCAP.CD

Millennium Challenge Corporation Country Scorecard

The Millennium Challenge Corporation, a U.S. Government entity charged with delivering development grants to countries that have demonstrated a commitment to reform, produced scorecards for countries with a per capita gross national income (GNI) or USD4,125 or less. A list of countries/economies with MCC scorecards and links to those scorecards is available here: http://www.mcc.gov/pages/selection/scorecards. Details on each of the MCC's indicators and a guide to reading the scorecards are available here: http://www.mcc.gov/pages/docs/doc/reportguide-to-the-indicators-and-the-selection-process-fy-2015.

2. Conversion and Transfer Policies

Foreign Exchange

Morocco guarantees full currency convertibility for capital transactions, free transfer of profits, and free repatriation of invested capital. Generally, the investors must notify the government of the investment transaction, providing the necessary legal and financial documentation. With respect to the cross-border transfer of investment proceeds to foreign investors, the rules vary depending on the type of investment.

A currency-convertibility regime is available to foreign investors, including Moroccans living abroad, who invest in Morocco. This regime facilitates their investments in Morocco, repatriation of income, and profits on investments. Foreign investments financed in foreign currency can be transferred tax-free, without amount or duration limits. This income can be dividends, attendance fees, rental income, benefits, and interests. Capital contributions made in convertible currency, contributions made by debit of forward convertible accounts, and net transfer capital-gains may also be repatriated. For the transfer of dividends, bonuses, or benefit shares, the investor must provide the balance sheets and profits and losses accounts, annexed documents relating to the fiscal year in which the transfer is requested, as well as the statement of extra-accounting adjustments made in order to obtain the taxable income.

Morocco has achieved relatively stable macroeconomic and financial conditions under an exchange rate peg, which has helped achieve price stability and insulate the economy from nominal shocks. The peg, which was set at an 80/20 split Euro/Dollar until April 2015, has recently been reallocated to a 60/40 Euro/Dollar basket, reflecting evolving trade relations. The IMF advocates a more flexible exchange rate, which would allow Morocco to respond better to shocks while improving the economy's competitiveness. The Central Bank has signaled its willingness to consider such a change but on a gradual basis.

Remittance Policies

Please refer to previous section for information applicable to remittances.

Morocco is a member of the Middle East and North Africa Financial Action Task Force. The 2014 International Narcotics Control Strategy Report (INCSR), Volume II: Money Laundering and Financial Crimes Country Database, classifies Morocco as a "jurisdiction of concern" http://www.state.gov/j/inl/rls/nrcrpt/2014/supplemental/227713.htm.

3. Expropriation and Compensation

Article 15 of the Moroccan Constitution stipulates that no expropriation can take place except in certain cases provided by law. The right to own property is guaranteed, but its extent and use may be restricted by law if the needs of economic and social planning and development require it.

U.S. Mission Morocco is not aware of any recent, confirmed instances of private property being expropriated for other than public purposes, or being expropriated in a manner that is discriminatory or not in accordance with established principles of international law.

4. Dispute Settlement

Legal System, Specialized Courts, Judicial Independence, Judgments of Foreign Courts

The Moroccan legal system is based on both civil law (French system) and Islamic law. The principal sources of commercial legislation in Morocco are the 1913 Dahir of Obligations and Contracts, as amended, and the 1996 Code of Commerce. Law No. 53-95 established Morocco's Commercial Courts. According to a Moroccan WTO submission: "This law gives these courts exclusive jurisdiction to hear trade disputes" . These courts also have sole competence to entertain industrial property disputes, as provided for in Law No. 17-97 on the Protection of Industrial Property, irrespective of the nature of the parties."

According to the European Bank for Reconstruction and Development's 2013 Morocco Country Assessment Report (http://www.ebrd.com/downloads/sector/legal/morocco.pdf), the establishment of special commercial courts in 1997 led to some improvement in the handling of commercial disputes. Nevertheless, the lack of training for judges on general commercial matters remains one of the key challenges to effective commercial dispute resolution in the country. In general, litigation procedures are time consuming and resource-intensive, and there is no legal requirement with respect to case publishing.

Bankruptcy

Morocco's bankruptcy law is based on French law. Commercial Courts have jurisdiction over all cases related to insolvency. The law follows the classical scheme in terms of protecting creditors, giving secured debtors priority claim on assets and proceeds over unsecured debtors, who in turn have priority over equity shareholders. Bankruptcy is not criminalized. The Ministry of Justice and Liberties (MOJL) is currently reviewing the national bankruptcy legislation. The draft law intends to shift the focus of bankruptcy from liquidation and restructuring to prevention and settlement.

The World Bank's 2015 Doing Business report ranked Morocco 113 out of 189 countries in "Resolving Insolvency" (down 5 positions from 2014).

Investment Disputes

In an effort to promote foreign investment, the Moroccan legislature has adopted laws to protect both foreign investors and their Moroccan counterparts. Morocco is a member of the International Center for the

Settlement of Investment Disputes (ICSID) and a party to the 1958 Convention on the Recognition and Enforcement of Foreign Arbitral Awards (with reservations) and the 1965 Convention on the Settlement of Investment Disputes between States and Nationals of Other states.

In general, investor rights are backed by an impartial procedure for dispute settlement that is transparent.

There have been no investment disputes involving a U.S. person in the last 10 years.

International Arbitration

Foreign companies have cited their ability to choose arbitration outside Morocco (in the case of litigation) as a strong benefit for doing business in the country.

Law No. 08-05 established a system of conventional arbitration and mediation, while allowing parties to apply the Code of Civil Procedure in their dispute resolution. Disputes may be brought before eight Commercial Courts, (located in Rabat, Casablanca, Fez, Tangier, Marrakech, Agadir, Oujda and Meknes) and three Commercial Courts of Appeal (located in Casablanca, Fez and Marrakech).

Arbitration is increasingly used in Morocco. The U.S. Agency for International Development (USAID) and the International Finance Corporation (IFC) worked with Morocco in 2008 and 2009 to establish a national commission on Alternative Dispute Resolution (ADR) with a mandate to regulate mediation training centers and develop mediator certification systems. The goal of this program was to increase the use of mediation in the prevention phase of bankruptcy proceedings and in the resolution of business disputes outside of the courts. Although the program remained limited in its implementation, the business community generally viewed early use of the system in Rabat and Casablanca as favorable.

There have been no claims brought by foreign investors under the investment chapter of the U.S.-Morocco Free Trade Agreement since it came into effect in 2006.

ICSID Convention and New York Convention

Morocco is a member of the International Center for Settlement of Investment Disputes (ICSID) and signed its convention in June 1967. Morocco is also party to the New York Convention of 1958 on the Recognition and Enforcement of Foreign Arbitral Awards.

Duration of Dispute Resolution

According to the Center of Arbitration and Mediation in Rabat, maximum duration of mediation cases per Moroccan law is six months, which is renewable. In reality, cases are usually solved in less than three months. In cases involving arbitration, Moroccan law does not proscribe any fixed period, but rather the duration of dispute resolution depends on the parties. In the most complex cases, arbitration can take 12-18 months. Regarding court resolutions, industry sources indicate that proceedings before commercial court take approximately 12 months, and the same at the appeal level. Court resolution duration can range from 2 to 10 plus years in some cases.

The main challenges to resolving disputes when litigated within local courts include inconsistencies of judgments; lack of dissemination of case-law; and inadequate training of magistrate, lawyers, legal experts, and judicial officers. Despite these challenges, justice reform is ongoing and is generating tangible improvements.

Morocco officially recognizes foreign arbitration awards. Domestic arbitration awards are also enforceable subject to an enforcement order issued by the president of the commercial court, who verifies that no elements of the award violate public order or the defense rights of the parties. As Morocco is a member of the New York Convention, international awards are also enforceable in accordance with the provisions of the said convention. Morocco is also a member of the Washington Convention for the International Centre for Settlement of Investment Disputes (ICSID), and as such agrees to enforce and uphold ICSID arbitral awards.

5. Performance Requirements and Investment Incentives

WTO/TRIMS

The WTO Trade Related Investment Measures' (TRIMs) database does not indicate any reported Moroccan measures to be inconsistent with TRIMs requirements. However, many measures, regarding public procurement for example, reportedly show preferences to companies utilizing local content or establishing local production facilities. The government also maintains several "free zones" in which companies enjoy lower tax rates and relaxed labor laws in exchange for an obligation to export at least 85 percent of their production. In some cases, the government provides generous incentives for companies to locate production facilities in the country but stipulates other requirements in return.

Investment Incentives

Morocco offers incentives designed to encourage foreign and local investment. Morocco's Investment Charter gives the same benefits to all investors regardless of the industry in which they operate (except agriculture, which remains outside the scope of the Charter.)

Morocco provides a range of investment incentives including:

- A corporate tax holiday during the first five years of business and a 17.5 percent rate thereafter.
- VAT exemptions: Equipment goods, materials, and tools needed to achieve investment projects involving an amount higher than or equal to 200 million dirhams (around USD 24 million) are exempt from VAT on imports, within the framework of an agreement concluded with the state, during a period of 36 months from the start of business.
- Import duty exemptions: Businesses that commit to making an investment of an amount higher than or equal to 200 million dirhams are exempt from import duties (applicable to goods, materials, and tools needed for their project and imported directly by the companies) within the framework of an agreement concluded with the state.

Morocco has six integrated industrial zones within the region of Tangier, each dedicated to a different sector of the economy, including car manufacturing and aeronautics. Morocco has set up many free zones to offer companies incentives ranging from tax breaks, subsidies, and reduced customs duties.

Additionally, businesses associated with Casablanca Finance City receive a variety of incentives, including exemption from corporate taxes for the first five years after receiving CFC status. Afterwards, companies will be taxed a reduced rate of 8.75 percent instead of the standard 17.5 percent tax on export turnovers. Companies with regional headquarters in the CFC pay a reduced ten percent rate on profits, versus the average 30 percent standard rate. Employees of CFC-status companies also benefit from reduced personal income tax rates. Other CFC advantages include administrative assistance. CFC-status companies benefit from expedited processing of work permit applications for their foreign employees, cutting wait times from six months to one week.

More details on investment incentives: http://www.invest.gov.ma/upload/documents/en_Doc_236.pdf.

Research and Development

U.S. companies successfully compete for Moroccan government tenders, with no exclusions for competing in research and development programs.

Performance Requirements

The Moroccan government allows the hiring of foreign employees at all levels, although the process for obtaining visas can take up to six months.

Data Storage

The Government of Morocco generally requires investors to use domestic content in goods or technologies, and some government-originated tenders have local content requirements, particularly in certain sectors (such as solar energy). Likewise, local regulation requires the release of source code for certain telecommunications hardware products.

6. Right to Private Ownership and Establishment

Private ownership is permitted in all but a few sectors, including the mining and agricultural sectors. Phosphate extraction is managed by state-owned corporation, OCP. In addition, private investment in mining operations in the Tafilalet and Figuig regions is currently restricted. However, the Ministry of Energy, Mines, Water, and Environment has drafted legislation to eliminate this restriction. Although foreigners are prohibited from owning and cultivating agricultural land, they can purchase it for non-agricultural purposes. Morocco has sought to encourage foreign investment in the agricultural sector by making land available to foreigners through leases of up to 99 years.

7. Protection of Property Rights Real Property

The World Bank's 2015 Doing Business Report ranked Morocco 115 out of 189 countries in 2015 (up 11 positions from 2014) on "Registering Property." Some of the report's metrics on registering property in Morocco are below:

Process: 8 procedures required Time to Register Property: 40 days Cost: 5.9% of property value Information on the procedures to register property: http://www.doingbusiness.org/data/exploreeconomies/morocco/#registering-property.

In rural areas, land tenure insecurity, the fragmentation of land ownership, and the common ownership of land inhibit economic growth. The rates of land titling and land rights registration are low.

Land and natural resource issues facing Morocco include: (1) lack of comprehensive policies governing land, water, forests and mineral resources; (2) underdeveloped legal frameworks and limited, ambiguous formal laws governing land and other natural resources; (3) a limited rural land market; (4) limited water; (5) undeveloped programs for participatory forest management; and (6) slow progress on women's rights of access to and control over land and natural resources.

USAID's report on Morocco's Property Rights: http://usaidlandtenure.net/sites/default/files/country-profiles/fullreports/USAID_Land_Tenure_Morocco_Profile.pdf.

Intellectual Property Rights

According to the 2014 International Property Rights (IPR) Index, Morocco ranks 54 out of 97 countries in protecting physical and intellectual property rights. In December 2004, the Moroccan Parliament passed amendments to its intellectual property legislation bringing it into compliance with its commitments under the WTO TRIPS Agreement. Morocco has been a member of the World Intellectual Property Organization (WIPO) since 1971. It is party to the Bern Copyright, Paris Industrial Property, and Universal Copyright Conventions; the Brussels Satellite Convention; and the Madrid, Nice, and Hague Agreements for the Protection of Intellectual Property.

Morocco is working with the U.S. to fulfill its commitments under the U.S.-Morocco FTA. The FTA contains strong intellectual property protections, which were incorporated in Moroccan intellectual property legislation in 2006.

In 2011, Morocco took the significant step of completing its accession to the Budapest treaty on patents and to the WIPO treaties on Copyright and Phonograms. In addition, it signed the Beijing Treaty on Audiovisual Performances in 2012. Morocco is also a signatory to the Anti- Counterfeiting Trade Agreement (ACTA), though it has not yet entered into force. The ACTA establishes an international framework that will assist parties in their efforts to effectively combat the infringement of IPR, in particular the proliferation of counterfeiting and piracy, which undermines legitimate trade and the sustainable development of the world economy. On December 18, 2014, Morocco approved a new intellectual property rights (IPR) law, 23.13, which seeks to streamline the regulation of patents, trademarks, and industrial design to conform to international standards. The law also improves IPR legal remedies and the enforcement capabilities of the Moroccan government.

The Ministry of Industry, Trade, Investment, and the Digital Economy oversees the Moroccan Office of Industrial and Commercial Property (OMPIC), which serves as a registry for intellectual property rights for patents and trademarks in the industrial and commercial sectors. In 2014, Morocco granted 1,096 patents, including 588 to non-residents; registered 11,709 trademarks, including 5,462 to non-residents; and recorded 1,167 industrial designs, including 436 to non-residents. The Ministry of Communications oversees the Moroccan Copyright Office (BMDA), which registers copyrights for literary and artistic works, including software.

Morocco has a non-discriminatory legal system that is accessible to foreign business. While criminal and civil courts can hear IPR-related cases, commercial courts, particularly those in the Casablanca region, are becoming adept at adjudicating patent, trademark, and copyright cases. Casablanca courts hear approximately 85 percent of counterfeiting cases in Morocco. From filing until judgment, the average case takes 18 months. The new IPR law expands these efforts by increasing penalties for violation of those rights and by better defining civil and criminal jurisdiction and legal remedies. It also sets in motion an accreditation system for patent attorneys in order to better systematize and regulate the practice of patent law.

Moroccan Customs, BMDA, and OMPIC have initiated campaigns to target Morocco's largest counterfeit manufacturers and importers. To support these efforts, OMPIC partnered with the Moroccan General Business Confederation (CGEM) to form the National Committee for Industrial Property and Anti-Counterfeiting (CONPIAC), a bridge between the public and private sectors. CONPIAC has been active in supporting research regarding counterfeiting in Morocco and sponsored public events to raise awareness of the problem.

CONPIAC estimates that counterfeiting in Morocco results in a loss for the economy of 6 - 12 billion dirhams (USD734 million - USD1.47 billion) or 0.7 to 1.3 percent of gross domestic product (GDP). Preliminary studies show that counterfeiting is highest in textiles, followed by leather products, electrical goods, automobile parts, and cosmetics. A 2013 CONPIAC study estimated that the government loses 1 billion dirhams (USD122 million) in tax revenue annually and that the economy loses 30,000 jobs due to counterfeiting.

Morocco is not listed on either USTR's Special 301 report or the notorious markets report. Nevertheless both software and DVD piracy are issues in Morocco. Moreover, while the IP registration system is fairly efficient and protection mechanisms are in place to defend these rights, enforcement is lacking and legal avenues constrained due to a lack of familiarity with IP law.

For additional information about treaty obligations and points of contact at local IP offices, please see WIPO's country profiles at http://www.wipo.int/directory/en/.

Resources for Rights Holders

Embassy point of contact: U.S. Consulate General Casablanca, Foreign Commercial Service: Brenda VanHorn (Brenda.VanHorn@trade.gov)

The American Chamber of Commerce (AmCham) in Morocco can provide a list of lawyers: http://www.amcham.ma/.

8. Transparency of the Regulatory System

The government of Morocco makes draft legislation, including those related to investment, available for public comment. Morocco's Decree 2-06-388 of February 5, 2007 sets the conditions and terms for public procurement. It provides a detailed framework for public procurement and conforms to the principles of good governance, which guide efforts on an international level. The 2007 Decree applies to central government and local authorities. Public enterprises and establishments can adopt their own specific regulations provided they comply with regulations regarding competition and transparency. The new mechanism seeks to encourage competition by introducing the principle of equal treatment for bidders in all phases of procurement and by requiring the contracting authority to provide adequate and equitable information to all competitors via the government procurement website.

Despite government efforts to increase the system's transparency, Morocco's administration is opaque and difficult to navigate. Routine permits, especially those required by local government agencies, can be difficult to obtain. Morocco has sought, with some success, to increase the transparency of its public tenders. However, recent moves to decentralize the procurement process have seen only limited implementation pending the government's general "regionalization" plan.

In 2006 a new charter for the central bank created an independent board of directors and prohibited the Ministry of Finance and Economy from borrowing from the central bank except in exceptional circumstances.

As noted above, the Competition Council and the Central Authority for the Prevention of Corruption have responsibility for improving public governance and advocating for further market liberalization.

According to the World Economic Forum's Global Competitiveness Report 2013-2014 (http://reports.weforum.org/global-competitiveness-report-2014- 2015/economies/#economy=MAR), the surveyed companies cite limited access to financing as the most problematic factor for doing business in Morocco, followed by inefficient government bureaucracy and inadequately educated workforce.

Morocco is a member of UNCTAD's international network of transparent investment procedures: http://rabat.eregulations.org/. On this site, foreign and national investors can find detailed information on administrative procedures applicable to investment and income generating operations including the number of steps, name and contact details of the entities and persons in charge of procedures, required documents and conditions, costs, processing time and legal bases justifying the procedures.

9. Efficient Capital Markets and Portfolio Investment

The Casablanca Stock Exchange (CSE,) founded in 1929 and re-launched as a private institution in 1993, is one of the few regional exchanges with no restrictions on foreign participation. With a market capitalization of $56 billion (per CSE's 2013 annual report) and 74 listed companies (as of April 2015), CSE is the third largest exchange in Africa. The market is currently dominated by institutional investors which act on long-term trends. Short-selling, which would enable investors to profit from the downward trend, is not allowed on the CSE at present.

The market in Morocco is shallow and illiquid compared to other emerging and frontier markets, with many large firms controlled by privately owned holding groups. The Morgan Stanley Capital International's (MSCI) 2012 Annual Market Classification Review announced in June 2012 Morocco's reclassification to "Frontier Markets" from "Emerging Market" status, where it remains, mainly due to its illiquidity. The report stated that, "the MSCI Morocco Index is more in line with the size and liquidity requirements of Frontier Markets following a significant decrease in liquidity since 2008, which resulted in a simultaneous decrease in the number of constituents in the MSCI Morocco Index."

The 1993 Law on the CSE has changed little over the years, and efforts are ongoing to further liberalize the management of the CSE and to empower the market regulator.

Money and Banking System, Hostile Takeovers

Morocco's banking system is one of the most liberalized in North Africa. Nonetheless, it is highly concentrated, with the six largest banks accounting for 85 percent of banking sector assets and access to finance, particularly for small and medium sized enterprises, remains challenging.

Credit is allocated on market terms, and foreign investors are able to obtain credit on the local market. There are some cross-shareholding arrangements, but they are not tailored to exclude foreign investment. The U.S. Mission has not received any reports of efforts by the private sector or industry to restrict foreign participation in standard-setting organizations. The government has actively sought out the participation of foreign investors for discussions on improving the business climate in Morocco.

In the 2013-2014 World Economic Forum's Global Competitiveness Report (http://reports.weforum.org/the-global-competitiveness-report-2013-2014/) Morocco dropped in ranking from 70 to 77 out of 148 countries. In the report's eighth pillar, "Financial Market Development," Morocco received a score of 4.6 (down from 4.8 a year before) for "availability of financial services" (where 1 = not at all; 7 = provides a wide variety). Morocco received a 2.8 (down from 3.2 a year before) for "ease of access to loans" (where 1 = difficult; 7 = easy). Morocco improved its score from a year before from 5.3 to

5.7 for "soundness of banks" (where 1 = insolvent and may require bailout; 7 = generally healthy with sound balance sheet). Morocco was ranked 41 out of 148 countries on soundness of banks.

Among the main legal reform projects for the banking sector is the creation of a new provision that will enable banks to specialize in offering Islamic products. These new banks, called participatory banks, will be supervised by the Sharia Financial Committee to ensure the products are sharia-compliant.

A new chapter called "macro-prudential supervision" is also being added to the current banking Law 34-03 to create a new governmental supervisory body (the Supervisory and Coordination Committee of Systemic Risks) to analyze the risks of the financial market.

10. COMPETITION FROM STATE-OWNED ENTERPRISES

Reform of the state-owned enterprise sector in Morocco has undergone three distinct phases: 1) structural reforms in the 1980s; 2) modernization of their environment in the 1990s; and 3) the liberalization of numerous industries in the 2000s.

The public enterprise portfolio consists of 241 state-owned enterprises (SOEs), 42 percent of which operate in productive sectors and 38 percent in the social domain, according to a 2012 report by the OECD (http://www.oecd.org/corporate/ca/corporategovernanceofstateownedenterprises/50087769.pdf). The Treasury has direct equity interest in 44 companies, 43 percent of which operate in the infrastructure sector. Act No. 69-00 on State Financial Control of Public Enterprises, adopted in 2003, defined Moroccan SOEs for the first time using three distinct categories: (1) state companies are those in which public bodies hold all the equity, (2) public subsidiaries are companies of which public bodies hold more than half the equity, and (3) semi-public companies are companies of which public bodies hold less than half of the equity.

Forty-nine percent of SOE firms are affiliated with three public holding companies (Caisse de Depot et de Gestion, OCP SA, and Banque Centrale Populaire); 119 are local or regional in scope; 53 have subsidiaries or affiliates abroad; and 11 are publicly traded.

Several sectors remain under public monopoly, managed either directly by public institutions (phosphate production, rail transport, some postal services, airport services) or by the municipalities (wholesale distribution of fruit and vegetables, fish, slaughterhouses). Several activities that were traditionally run by the government are now open to private domestic or foreign operators, under the delegated management or concession arrangements generally subject to tendering procedures. This is the case, for example, with water and electricity distribution, construction and operation of motorways, and the management of non-hazardous wastes.

Morocco is not party to the WTO Government Procurement Agreement.

OECD Guidelines on Corporate Governance of SOEs

The Moroccan National Commission on Corporate Governance was established in 2007. It prepared the first Moroccan Code of Good Corporate Governance Practices in 2008. Based on the OECD Principles of Corporate Governance, it applies to both the private and public sectors. Recognizing the specific features of the SOE sector, the Commission drafted in 2011 a code dedicated to state-owned enterprises, drawing on the OECD Guidelines on Corporate Governance of SOEs. The code, which came into effect in 2012, is aimed at enhancing SOE's overall performance. It requires greater use of standardized public procurement and accounting rules, outside audits, the inclusion of independent directors, board evaluations, greater transparency, and better disclosure.

Moroccan SOEs are overseen by boards of directors or supervisory boards. These bodies are governed by the Financial Control Act and the Limited Liability Companies Act. The Ministry of Economy and Finance's Department of Public Enterprises and Privatization monitors SOE governance. Pursuant to Act No. 69-00, SOE annual accounts are publicly available. Under Act No. 62-99, or the Financial Jurisdictions Code, the Court of Accounts and the Regional Courts of Accounts audit the management of a number of public enterprises.

Currently, a number of governance-related initiatives are a priority. These include an initiative that aims to help SOEs contribute to the emergence of regional development clusters. The government is also attempting to improve the use of multi-year contracts with major SOEs as tool to enhance performance and transparency.

Sovereign Wealth Funds

Morocco currently does not have a sovereign wealth fund.

11. Corporate Social Responsibility

Corporate social responsibility (CSR) has gained strength in tandem with Morocco's economic expansion and stability. The country's businesses are slowly taking responsibility for the impact of their activities on the environment, communities, employees and consumers. For example, CGEM has awarded "social labels" to companies based on a systematic analysis of the effects of their activities. The Moroccan Association of Textile and Apparel Industries also award a "Fibre Citoyenne" label to socially worthy companies. Additionally, Morocco launched the UN Global Compact network in 2006 in Casablanca. The project provides support to companies who affirm their commitment to social responsibility. The major trade unions (CDT, UMT, UGMT, and FDT) and CGEM were among its initial members. Maroc Telecom joined in November 2012, demonstrating its commitment to adhere to the Compact's principles in the area of human rights, labor law, environment, and corruption.

AmCham in Morocco has five committees, including one that promotes good corporate citizenship and social responsibility. The committee focuses on recognizing excellence in CSR of AmCham members. The committee also develops public-private sector partnerships and implements programs that have an educational, philanthropic, and/or socially responsible nature within the broader context of U.S.-Morocco economic relations.

OECD Guidelines for Multinational Enterprises

While there is no legislation mandating specific levels of CSR, foreign and some local enterprises follow generally accepted principles such as the OECD CSR guidelines for multinational companies. NGOs are also taking an increasingly active role in monitoring corporations' CSR performance. Morocco's national contact point is the Moroccan Investment Agency (www.invest.gov.ma).

12. Political Violence

Morocco is a monarchy with a constitution, government, Parliament and judiciary, in which ultimate power and authority rest with the King. A process of qualified democratic reform is underway, and the country is broadly regarded as politically stable. The U.S. government maintains excellent relations with Morocco and designated Morocco a Major Non-NATO Ally in 2004. A series of terrorist bombings in Casablanca in March 2003, March and April 2007, as well as the bombing of the Argana Café in Marrakesh in April 2011, underscore that Morocco continues to face a terrorist threat. Counterterrorism cooperation is excellent. The Moroccan Government aggressively investigates terrorist suspects and has dismantled a number of terrorist cells over the past years.

Demonstrations occur frequently in Morocco and usually center on domestic issues. Most demonstrations have been peaceful and orderly. There are infrequent reports of anti-American sentiment and isolated instances of violence. In September 2012, protesters held demonstrations in Casablanca in response to the video, The Innocence of Muslims, produced in the U.S. The largest turnout of the two demonstrations consisted of 200 - 300 protesters who gathered near the U.S. Consulate.

During periods of heightened regional tension, large demonstrations may take place in major cities. Additionally, the Arab Spring of 2011 led to the creation of the February 20th Movement in Morocco. This disparate group of protesters took to the street in numbers of between a few hundred to tens of thousands almost every Sunday from its inception through March 2012. It has since attempted to inspire new popular protests, but attendance is often low. Unions and labor groups occasionally organize public demonstrations to protest working conditions, salary levels, or other social benefit issues.

The sparsely settled Western Sahara was the site of armed conflict between the Moroccan government and the POLISARIO Front, which demands independence. A cease-fire has been in effect since 1991, but sovereignty over the territory remains disputed. Negotiations to reach a settlement resumed in 2007 under UN auspices, but the dispute hampers development in the territory, as well as economic and political integration in the North Africa region.

13. Corruption

According to the 2013 State Department's Country Report on Human Rights Practices, Moroccan law provides criminal penalties for official corruption, but the government does not implement the law effectively. Officials often engage in corrupt practices with impunity. Corruption is a serious problem in the executive branch, including police, as well as the legislative and judicial branches of government. There have been reports of government corruption and several notable prosecutions. In July 2013 courts sentenced the director general of the National Airports Office to five years in prison for embezzlement of public funds. Observers generally consider corruption a serious problem, particularly among magistrates. In 2013, courts sentenced magistrates from Kenitra, Taza, Meknes, and Inezgane to prison terms for corruption. The King, who has made statements calling for judicial system reform since 2009, acknowledged the judiciary's lack of independence and susceptibility to influence. Many members of the well-entrenched and conservative judicial community are loath to adopt new procedures.

The Central Commission for the Prevention of Corruption (ICPC) is the agency responsible for combating corruption but lacks authority to require responses from government institutions. An implementing law that will give it expanded authorities to conduct investigations of corruption is forthcoming. In 2010 ICPC set up an internet portal for civil society and small businesses to identify instances of corruption: www.stopcorruption.ma. ICPC also publishes quarterly reports covering specific cases of corruption and the outcome of any subsequent prosecution. ICPC acknowledges that the anticorruption situation has not improved significantly and that governmental policy continues to lack a strategic dimension and effective commitment.

In addition to ICPC, MOJL and the government accountability court have jurisdiction over corruption issues but have pursued no high-profile cases. The inspector general of MOJL investigated 107 ethics complaints against judges in 2012, which resulted in the referral of three judges to the Supreme Judicial Council for disciplinary measures.

Observers have noted that there is widespread corruption in the police force. The government claims to investigate corruption and other instances of police malfeasance through an internal mechanism. In one widely publicized investigation in 2014, 24 police officers in Casablanca were presented with a choice between resigning or facing justice on charges of corruption, with the majority choosing resignation. In general, authorities did not provide official information on the results of the investigations.

ntina, Austria, Bahrain, Benin, Belgium-Luxembourg Economic ulgaria, Burkina Faso, Cameroon, Central African Republic, Chad, roatia, Czech Republic, Denmark, Dominican Republic, Egypt, El Equatorial Guinea, Estonia, Finland, France, Gabon, Gambia, Greece, Guinea, Hungary, India, Indonesia, Iran, Islamic Republic Italy, Jordan, Korea, Republic of, Kuwait, Lebanon, Libya, a, The former Yugoslav Republic of, Malaysia, Mauritania, ds, Oman, Pakistan, Poland, Portugal, Qatar, Romania, Senegal, Serbia, Slovakia, Spain, Sudan, Sweden, Switzerland, Syrian Arab Tunisia, Turkey, Ukraine, United Arab Emirates, United Kingdom, tes of America, Vietnam, Yemen.

cco's BITs: http://investmentpolicyhub.unctad.org/IIA/CountryBits/ erMenu

.S. and Morocco signed a BIT on July 22, 1985, but its provisions med by the investment chapter of the U.S.-Morocco FTA, which o force on January 1, 2006. The BIT's dispute settlement provisions effect for ten years after the effective date of the FTA for certain s and investment disputes which predate the Agreement.

nent Chapter of the FTA: http://www.ustr.gov/sites/default/ s/agreements/fta/morocco/asset_upload_file651_38 38.pdf

Taxation Treaties

S. signed an income tax treaty with Morocco in 1977: http://www. irs-trty/morocco.pdf.

15. OPIC and Other Investment Insurance Programs

o signed an agreement with OPIC in 1961. The agreement was 1995 and ratified by the Moroccan parliament in June 2004. The can be found here: http://www.opic.gov/sites/default/files/ Morocco-1995.pdf.

st 2013, OPIC provided its consent for a new $40 million, eight-an facility with Attijariwafa Bank to support loans to small and d enterprises (SMEs) in Morocco under a risk sharing agreement

See more at: http://www.state.gov/j/drl/rls/hrr[
.htm#wrapper.

In the 2014 Corruption Perception Index p
International (TI) (http://www.libertadciuda
2013_CPIBrochure_EN.pdf), Morocco ranked 80
improvement of 11 places over its 2013 rank.
criticized the Index, which reflects public percept
for not emphasizing recent anti-corruption effort
the transparency of public tenders and implemen
senior government officials declare their assets a
government service.

The latest TI report on Morocco: ht
cpi2014/results.

UN Anticorruption Convention, OECD C Bribery

UN Anticorruption Convention:

Morocco signed the UN Convention agai
hosted the States Parties to the Convention's Fou

Morocco has published its anti-corruption
invest.gov.ma/upload/documents/en_Doc_223.p

Resources to Report Corruption

Instance Centrale de Prévention de la Corru
Avenue Annakhil, Immeuble High Tech, Ha
Hay Ryad-Rabat
Tél.: 05 37 57 86 60
Fax: 05 37 71 16 73
E-mail: contact@icpc.ma
Transparency International National Chapt
+212-522-542-699
http://www.transparencymaroc.ma/index.p

14. BILATERAL INVESTME

Morocco has signed Bilateral Investn
following 75 countries:

Arg
Union,
China, C
Salvador
Germany
of, Iraq
Macedon
Netherla
Senegal,
Republic
United St

Moro
142#iiaIn

The
were subs
entered in
remain in
investmen

Inves
files/uploa

Bilatera

The U
irs.gov/pu

Moroc
updated in
agreement
docs/africa

In Aug
year term l
medium-siz

between OPIC and Citi Maghreb. In August 2014, OPIC signed an additional agreement with Attijariwafa and Wells Fargo to provide additional support to SMEs. OPIC has a long history of supporting projects in Morocco and has provided finance or insurance support to 22 deals over the past four decades. This recent agreement between Citi Maghreb and OPIC is OPIC's first risk-sharing agreement for the banking sector in Morocco.

16. LABOR

Morocco is in a paradoxical situation: large numbers of graduates are unable to find jobs commensurate with their education and training, while employers complain of skills shortages and mismatches. According to some U.S. companies in Morocco, qualified labor is not only rare, but also expensive, with wages equivalent to those in France.

In 2012 the World Bank described the problem of youth unemployment in Morocco as "very serious." Youth (aged 15 to 29) make up about 30 percent of Morocco's total population and 44 percent of the working age population (aged 15 to 64). According to a June 2012 World Bank report, Moroccan youth are largely excluded from the sustained economic growth the country has experienced in the last decade.

World Bank report: http://www.youthpolicy.org/national/Morocco_2012_Youth_Report.pdf.

The national unemployment rate for the third quarter of 2014 was 9.6 percent (up from 9.1 percent from the same period last year) with urban unemployment reaching 14.5 percent compared to 4.1 percent rural unemployment. Nationally 20.6 percent of youth aged 15-24 were unemployed, and 13.6 percent of those aged 25-34 were unemployed. The unemployment rate of university graduates was 20 percent. Unemployment rates are disproportionately higher for graduates from universities, secondary schools, and vocational training institutions that have open enrollment.

Source: Haut Commissariat au Plan http://www.hcp.ma.

Lowering youth unemployment is a government priority since high youth unemployment has historically resulted in serious social and political tensions. Moreover, without a trained workforce capable of increasing productivity, Morocco cannot generate sufficient prosperity through private-sector growth.

USAID is launching a $38 million project to address this challenge and enhance the employability of young Moroccans. The project will help university and vocational students' transition from school to work by building stronger links between education institutions and the private sector.

According to the State Department's Country Report on Human Rights Practices (http://www.state.gov/j/drl/rls/hrrpt/humanrightsreport/index.htm# wrapper), the Moroccan constitution grants workers the right to form and join unions, strike, and bargain collectively, with some restrictions (S 396-429 Labor Code Act 1999, No. 65/99). The law prohibits certain categories of government employees, including members of the armed forces, police, and some members of the judiciary, from forming and joining unions and from conducting strikes. The labor code does not cover domestic workers.

The law concerning strikes requires compulsory arbitration of disputes, prohibits sit-ins, calls for a ten-day notice of a strike, and allows for the hiring of replacement workers. The government may intervene in strikes. The government generally respects freedom of association and the right to collective bargaining. Labor disputes (S 549-581 Labor Code Act 1999, No. 65/99) are common and in some cases result in employers failing to implement collective bargaining agreements and withholding wages. Trade unions complain that the government at times uses Article 288 of the penal code to prosecute workers for striking and to suppress strikes.

Once strong and politically influential, the Moroccan trade union movement is now fragmented and no longer possesses the political clout it had 50 years ago when it helped lead the country to independence. Nevertheless, five of the more than 25 trade union federations remain strong enough to wield some political influence. Although unions claim high membership rates (Morocco has about 600,000 unionized workers), less than six percent of the 11.26 million person workforce.

Investors continue to view labor regulations as a significant constraint. They complain that procedures regarding lay-offs remain complicated and onerous, imposing a significant financial burden on companies. Rules regarding foreign personnel are also vague and can lead to conflicting interpretations and arbitrary decisions.

Morocco's labor code prohibits all forms of forced or compulsory labor. Penalties for forced labor include a fine for the first offense and jail term of up to three months for subsequent offences. The minimum age for employment in all sectors is 15 (S 143 Labor Code Act 1999, No. 65/99). The law prohibits any employee from working more than 10 hours per day except under specific circumstances.

Morocco's minimum wage for the industrial sector (SMIG) was recently renegotiated and will increase by ten percent to 13.46 DH/hour (or USD

1.66/hour) by July 2015. While the minimum wage will increase consumer purchasing power, many in the business community fear a loss of competitiveness. According to Morocco's business association CGEM, minimum wage has increased annually between 2001 and 2012 by 9.7 percent while inflation has increased by 1.7 percent. In exchange for the increase in minimum wage, CGEM has asked for the government to update its regulation on strikes and the Labor Code.

Morocco has ratified the following International Labor Organization (ILO) conventions: Forced Labor Convention (1957); Right to Organize and Collective Bargaining (1957); Equal Remuneration (1979); Abolition of Forced labor (1966); Discrimination-Employment and Occupation (1963); Minimum Age (2000); and the Worst Forms of Child Labor Convention (2001). Morocco has yet to ratify the Freedom of Association and Protection of the Right to Organize Convention.

For a list of the 62 ILO conventions Morocco has ratified, see here: http://www.ilo.org/dyn/normlex/en/f?p=1000:11200:0::NO:11200:P11200_COUNTRY_ID:102 993.

17. Foreign Trade Zones/Free Ports/ Trade Facilitation

Instituted by Law 19-94 (Dahir No. 1-95-1 dated January 26, 1995), export processing zones are identified areas of the customs territory where industrial and commercial export activities are exempted from customs regulations, foreign trade and exchange control. Each zone is created and defined by a decree which stipulates the nature and activities of the companies that can operate in the zone.

Free zones in Morocco include: Nouaceur Free Zone in Casablanca; Tanger Free Zone; Tanger Automotive City; Tetouan Shore; Oujda Free Zone; and the Atlantic Free Zone.

Detailed information on Morocco's free zones (in French): http://www.ilo.org/wcmsp5/groups/public/@ed_dialogue/@actrav/documents/publication/wcms _183548.pdf.

General information on Morocco's free zones (in English): http://www.invest.gov.ma.

18. Foreign Direct Investment and Foreign Portfolio Investment Statistics

Table 2. Key Macroeconomic Data, U.S. FDI in Host Country/Economy

	*Host Country Statistical source**		*USG or international statistical source*		*USG or International Source of Data: BEA; IMF; Eurostat; UNCTAD, Other*
Economic Data	*Year*	*Amount*	*Year*	*Amount*	
Host Country Gross Domestic Product (GDP) ($M USD)	2013	103.8	2013	99.4	www.worldbank.org/en/country
Foreign Direct Investment	*Host Country Statistical source**		*USG or international statistical source*		*USG or internationalSource of data: BEA; IMF; Eurostat; UNCTAD, Other*
U.S. FDI in partner country ($MUSD, stock positions)	2012	217.72	2013	599	http://bea.gov/international/factsheet/factsheet.cfm?Area=426
Host country's FDI in the United States ($M USD, stock positions)	n/a	n/a	2013	-15	http://bea.gov/international/factsheet/factsheet.cfm?Area=426
Total inbound stock of FDI as % host GDP	n/a	n/a	2013	1.0%	

* Local source for GDP: Bank Al-Maghrib (http://www.bkam.ma/).

Table 3. Sources and Destination of FDI

Data listed below is from 2013 and sourced from the IMF's Coordinated Direct Investment Survey (CDIS). Data from the Moroccan Investment Development Agency from 2014 indicates a 52% drop in direct investments from France, an 88.7% rise in U.S. direct investments, and a 69.1% increase in Saudi Arabian investments. Emirati investments remained steady, rising just 5.5%.

Outward direct investment data from Morocco is not available from the IMF, which relies on country authorities to submit data for this survey.

Direct Investment from/in Counterpart Economy Data					
From Top Five Sources/To Top Five Destinations *(US Dollars, Millions)*					
Inward Direct Investment		Outward Direct Investment			
Total Inward	22,293	100%	Total Outward	n/a	100%
France	15,171	68%			
United Arab Emirates	1,628	7%			
Spain	1,115	5%			
Kuwait	820	4%			
The Netherlands	797	4%			

"0" reflects amounts rounded to +/- USD 500,000.

Table 4. Sources of Portfolio Investment

Portfolio Investment Assets						
Top Five Partners (Millions, US Dollars)						
Total		Equity Securities		Total Debt Securities		
All Countries	22,293	100%	All Countries n/a	100%	All Countries n/a	100%
France	15,171	68%				
UAE	1,628	7%				
Spain	1,115	5%				
Kuwait	820	4%				
Netherlands	797	4%				

Source: IMF Coordinated Portfolio Investment Survey.

19. Contact for More Information

Contact Point at Post for Public Inquiries:
Until September 1, 2015:
Christopher Wilken.
Senior Commercial Officer.
U.S. Consulate General, Casablanca.
+212 522 264 550.
Christopher.Wilken@trade.gov.
After September 1, 2015 Brenda VanHorn.
Senior Commercial Officer Brenda.VanHorn@trade.gov.
U.S. Consulate General, Casablanca
+212 522 264 550 Brenda.VanHorn@trade.gov.

INDEX

#

A

B

C

D

E

H

I

J

K

L

M

N

O

P

Q

R

S

T

U

V

W

Y